"This book will help you understand yourself and point the way to having healthier responses. Every married couple will profit from the message of this book."

—**Gary Chapman, PhD, author of**
The 5 Love Languages

"*The Mindful Marriage* contains insights and practical tools to help you transform intimacy in your relationship. It blends a powerful combination of research-based techniques, biblical truth, and real-life application."

—**Dr. Juli Slattery, author of**
God, Sex, and Your Marriage

"What a unique, engaging, self-revealing presentation! Readers will be able to relate personally to the concepts as they are gently guided through this mindfully healing process."

—**Dr. Cliff Penner and Joyce Penner,**
authors of *The Gift of Sex*

"Ron and Nan Deal's deep understanding of neuroscience and how our brains can truly be rewired for love and peace, as well as their foundation of a biblical lens, is a great contribution to this arena. These principles can revolutionize marriages that seem hopeless, as well as make a good marriage even better. Highly recommended!"

—**John Townsend, PhD, author of thirty-five**
books, including the *New York Times*
bestselling Boundaries book series

"In this insightful book, the Deals and Hargraves show us how to set aside our prideful tendencies and focus on loving our spouse the way God intends. I'm confident that successfully applying these principles will transform your relationship."

—Greg Smalley, PhD, vice president, marriage and family formation, Focus on the Family

"*The Mindful Marriage* is groundbreaking in how it synthesizes what we know about interpersonal neurobiology, attachment research, and self-control to transform partners by the renewing of their minds. Practical and transformative, I highly recommend this book."

—Steve Arterburn, bestselling author and founder of New Life Live!

"It's powerful. Practical. And breathtakingly honest. Ron and Nan beautifully share their own intimate journey toward restoration and resilience. This book is a treasure trove of wisdom for anyone looking to deepen their relationship through mindful intentions."

—Drs. Les and Leslie Parrott, *New York Times* bestselling authors of *Saving Your Marriage Before It Starts*

"I love this book! Therapists and ministers should have this book on their shelf and get it into the hands of every marriage person they know."

—Chris Gonzalez, PhD

"This book will be an indispensable guide for couples and the therapists who work with them."

—**Mark A. Yarhouse, PsyD,
professor, Wheaton College**

"*The Mindful Marriage* is a deep calling, not only in marriage, but across every relationship. It is an honest, transparent, and compelling journey on how God sees beauty in brokenness. A must read."

—**Eric Scalise, PhD, professor,
Lipscomb University**

"This accessible, engaging book is designed and ready to change your marriage for the better."

—**Scott Symington, PhD, author of
*Freedom from Anxious Thoughts and Feelings***

"This insightful book offers practical guidance and profound wisdom, empowering partners to navigate their relationship with clarity and purpose. We highly recommend every couple grab a copy and embark on a journey towards a more mindful, fulfilling, and peaceful marriage."

—**Casey and Meygan Caston,
cofounders of Marriage365.com**

"This is a book, and manual, that I will recommend to both friends and clients."

—**Brad D. Strawn, PhD professor,
Fuller Seminary**

"*The Mindful Marriage* will be a game changer for couples! *The Mindful Marriage* walks you through an experience that helps you show up as the best version of you in your marriage and in life."

—**Julie M. Baumbardner, senior director of WinShape Marriage**

"With powerful stories and simple strategies, the Hargraves and Deals masterfully lead us on a pathway to peace and deep connection in our most important relationship—our marriage. This book is an essential!"

—**Dee Dee Mayer, senior director of RelateStrong, founder of Restoring Hope Therapy**

"Ron and Nan Deal draw from their personal journey and professional expertise to offer real practical strategies that can transform your marriage—and you."

—**Dr. Tim Clinton, president of the American Association Christian Counselors**

"This book will help you discover the why behind the pain— and then the actual, practical steps that will help you work through it and arrive at peace and togetherness for a lifetime."

—**Shaunti Feldhahn, social researcher and bestselling author of *For Women Only* and *For Men Only***

"If you have been wondering why you and your spouse relate to each other the way you do and how you can make lasting change, the answer to your question and a path forward is in this book!"

—John McGee, director of Watermark Resources and creator of the Re-engage marriage program

"Break the cycle of pain and build a stronger 'us' with the practical steps in *The Mindful Marriage*. It's time to transform your relationship."

—Michael Sytsma, PhD, founder of Building Intimate Marriages

"*The Mindful Marriage* is a biblical and practical road map to building (or rebuilding) the marriage you've dreamed of."

—Dave and Ashley Willis, authors and hosts of *The Naked Marriage* podcast

"A blend of psychology, pastoral care, insights into modern neuroscience, and practical advice, this book will help you regulate yourself and bring new hope, passion, and power into your marriage."

—W. Lee Warren, MD, neurosurgeon, award-winning author, host of *The Dr. Lee Warren Podcast*

"This is a GREAT book for your marriage. It's insightful, practical, and yet deeper than most marriage books. I instantly became a believer in 'Restoration Therapy,' and so will you."

—Jim Burns, PhD, founder of HomeWord, host of the *HomeWord with Jim Burns* podcast

"This is the marriage book you've been looking for!"
—Nicole Zasowski, author of
What If It's Wonderful?

"Any couple wanting a stronger, more loving marriage should read *The Mindful Marriage.*"
—Nicky and Sila Lee, founders of The Marriage Course

The
Mindful
Marriage

Other Books by Ron Deal

Building Love Together in Blended Families (with Gary Chapman)

Daily Encouragement for the Smart Stepfamily (with Dianne Neal Matthews)

Dating and the Single Parent

Preparing to Blend

The Smart Stepdad

The Smart Stepfamily

The Smart Stepfamily DVD

The Smart Stepfamily Guide to Financial Planning (with Greg S. Pettys and David O. Edwards)

The Smart Stepfamily Participant's Guide

The Smart Stepfamily Marriage (and Study Guide) (with David H. Olson)

The Smart Stepmom (with Laura Petherbridge)

Other Books by Terry Hargrave

Boomers on the Edge

5 Days to a New Marriage (with Shawn Stoever)

Loving Your Parents When They Can No Longer Love You

Strength and Courage for Caregivers

Academic Publications by Terry Hargrave

Restoration Therapy: Understanding and Guiding Healing in Marriage and Family Therapy (with Franz Pfitzer)

Advances and Techniques in Restoration Therapy (with Nicole E. Zasowski & Miyoung Yoon Hammer)

The Essential Humility of Marriage

Forgiving the Devil: Coming to Terms with Damaged Relationships

Families and Forgiveness, 2nd Edition (with Nicole E. Zasowski)

The New Contextual Therapy (with Franz Pfitzer)

The Aging Family (with Suzanne Midori Hanna)

Finishing Well: Aging and Reparation in the Intergenerational Family (with William T. Anderson)

Books by Terry and Sharon Hargrave

5 Days to a New Self

RelateStrong Leader Guide for Couples

RelateStrong Leader Guide for Individuals (with Meghan Eaken)

The Mindful Marriage

Create Your Best Relationship Through Understanding and Managing Yourself

RON and NAN DEAL

with

TERRY and SHARON HARGRAVE

New York • Nashville

Worthy
Hachette Book Group
1290 Avenue of the Americas, New York, NY 10104
worthypublishing.com
@WorthyPub

First edition: January 2025

Worthy is a division of Hachette Book Group, Inc. The Worthy name and logo are registered trademarks of Hachette Book Group, Inc.

The publisher is not responsible for websites (or their content) that are not owned by the publisher.

The Hachette Speakers Bureau provides a wide range of authors for speaking events. To find out more, go to hachettespeakersbureau.com or email HachetteSpeakers@hbgusa.com.

Worthy Books may be purchased in bulk for business, educational, or promotional use. For information, please contact your local bookseller or the Hachette Book Group Special Markets Department at special.markets@hbgusa.com.

Scripture quotations marked RSV are from the Revised Standard Version of the Bible, copyright © 1946, 1952, and 1971 National Council of the Churches of Christ in the United States of America. Used by permission. All rights reserved worldwide.

Scripture marked NLT is taken from the *Holy Bible, New Living Translation*, copyright © 1996. Used by permission of Tyndale House Publishers, Inc., Wheaton, Illinois, 60189. All rights reserved.

Library of Congress Cataloging-in-Publication Data

Names: Deal, Ron L., author. | Deal, Nan, author.
Title: The mindful marriage : create your best relationship through understanding and managing yourself / Ron and Nan Deal.
Description: First edition. | New York, NY : Worthy Books, 2025. | Includes bibliographical references.
Identifiers: LCCN 2024034086 | ISBN 9781546007388 (hardcover) | ISBN 9781546007401 (ebook)
Subjects: LCSH: Marriage—Religious aspects—Christianity.
Classification: LCC BV835 .D399 2025 | DDC 248.8/44—dc23/eng/20240909
LC record available at https://lccn.loc.gov/2024034086

ISBNs: 9781546007388 (hardcover), 9781546007401 (ebook)

Printed in the United States of America

LSC-C

Printing 1, 2024

From Ron and Nan

*To Terry: Thank you for being there
when the bottom dropped out.*

*To Terry and Sharon: Thank you for your
friendship and confidence that we could help
put the cookies on the bottom shelf.*

*To Braden, Liz, and Austin, Connor, Brennan,
and any future grandchildren: Having you as our
family is eternal joy. This is the book about relationships
we wanted to write for you. We hope the truths found
here bless you as much as they have us.*

From Terry and Sharon

*To Ron and Nan and all the couples who have
chosen to share their stories with us: Because of you,
the generations that follow will understand the joy of
commitment and the gift of growing strong together.*

Authors' Note

Dear Readers,

The most important thing about you is not what you have done, where you have been, how much money you have, or how many followers you have.

What matters is *who* you follow.

May this book help you become more loving, trustworthy, and humble like Jesus.

Contents

Foreword

Dr. Terry Hargrave and Sharon Hargrave

It was, perhaps, the wisest statement ever made to us about the marriage relationship. Dr. Carl Whitaker, the well-known clinician and one of the founders of the field of marriage and family therapy, and I were scheduled to do a keynote for the American Association for Marriage and Family Therapy in 1991—I as a young man of thirty-three years and married for a decade; Carl, eighty years old and married for fifty-three years. During the frenetic lunch when we were supposed to be talking about aging and the family, Carl blurted out, "You know Terry, I love my wife, Muriel." Stunned, because the comment came totally out of the blue, I said haltingly, "Well, that is great, Carl." He went on. "But you know, as much as I would miss Muriel if she died, what I would miss more is what we are together."

There it was. The defining moment of our marriage, for our coupleness and for our relationship. It is what Carl used to refer to as "we-ness," what we have come to call "usness." Usness, in short, is what we are together. In other words, marriage is not about two people learning how to manage together and build a life together. It is not about meeting each other's needs and accomplishing tasks. It is not even about loving each other as individuals. Though a marriage is all of that, what Carl rocked us with that day was a new understanding of the essence of marriage as two people creating a whole new person—a whole new identity. An invisible but real "us." There is a Terry. There is a Sharon. And then there is what we are together. There is us.

It is important to realize we are not talking about a concept or an opinion. Us is a real, living being much in the same way the church is real and is the combined invisible entity of Jesus and His followers. In a way, the perfect metaphor for us is our children. Each of our children inherited half of their chromosomes from Sharon and half from Terry. When those chromosomes are combined in the magic of conception, the child becomes a whole new human being. Sure, our children and our usness have characteristics that are similar to both Terry and Sharon, but there is no doubt our children and our us have their own individual beings with their own personalities, likes and dislikes and patterns of growth.

More than anything else, caring for our marriage is like caring for a child. The two parents think first about the needs and well-being of the child long before they consider their own needs and wants. The same is true for our usness. Parents lavish their child with encouragement, nurture, and resources even though the child does not have the know-how or the inkling to do the same for the parents. The same is true for our usness. And most important, when the child falls short, disappoints, or fails, the parents align themselves with love, safety, and forgiveness to grow and patiently try again with the child. The same is true for our usness. The great conservative columnist George Will once said, "Biologically, adults produce children. Spiritually, children produce adults. Most of us do not grow up until we have helped children to do so. Thus, the generations form a braided cord." The same is true for our usness.

We make vows to one another to love, cherish, and to be there for better or worse, for richer or poorer, in sickness and in health. We tend to think of it as some kind of bargain between ourselves and our spouses: "I will take care of you if you take care of me." Nothing can be further from the truth.

When we speak vows, we are actually making our partner a blood relative by our spoken words. It is the same way we are grafted into the body of Jesus by our confession of sin and our recognition of who He is and what He has done for us. It is, both with our spouse and with the Holy God, the making of a relationship spoken into existence by our words, vows, commitments, and hearts. Oh yes, it is invisible, but it is real. It is us. And as we care for, nurture, and sacrifice for our "us" relationship, we actually find that we as individuals grow emotionally, cognitively, and spiritually.

This is the challenge of writing a book like *The Mindful Marriage*. We all—Ron and Nan Deal, and Sharon and Terry Hargrave—really desire for you and your spouse to have less conflict, more nurturing and loving moments, and more constructive time working together. But we also know that these things do not happen within you if your spouse becomes less selfish or faces their issues. These worthy goals happen when both of you are becoming more loving, nurturing, and giving. The truth is—and this is an encouraging truth—that this loving, nurturing, and giving self is already there inside of you. It comes out when you are settled in safety, confident in being loved, and able to deploy your gifts and talents freely. In short, it comes out of you when you are *emotionally regulated*. It shows up when you are being your best self or what the scripture calls your new self. It is recognizable to you and to your spouse and is likely the parts of both of you that attracted you to each other in the first place. But learning how to stay emotionally regulated—this is the challenge for all of us and the big task ahead of you in reading this book.

You and your spouse's usness can be emotionally triggered into dysregulation in a New York minute so instead of feeling safe and confident and using your gifts and talents, you are running out of control with feelings of being unloved and unsafe and taking actions that are demeaning, damaging, and destructive to your usness. Paul warns us of this triggering and emotional dysregulation in Ephesians 4:20–24:

> But that is not the way you learned Christ!—assuming that you have heard about him and were taught in him, as the truth is in Jesus, to put off your old self, which belongs to your former manner of life and is corrupt through deceitful desires, and to be renewed in the spirit of your minds, and to put on the new self, created after the likeness of God in true righteousness and holiness. (ESV)

When you are in your "old self," you are running your relationship by the old rules and the old ways of *the worst part of who you are and how you act*. When you are in your "new self," indeed you are becoming more of *your best self*. And as Paul clearly stated two thousand years before neuropsychology told us the same thing—you take off this old destructive self and put on the nurturing new self by *mindfulness*, or *the renewing of your mind*.

This is what this book is all about: helping you and your spouse do the good work of learning how to nurture, care for, and grow up in your usness while you engage in the wonderful practice of learning about yourself and the power you have to change. In reality, it is nothing more and nothing less than learning how to be a faithful follower of Jesus and living by the fruits of the Spirit through emotional regulation, practice, and discipleship. And yes, it will change everything about your marriage, your invisible usness, and the reality of what the two of you stand for in the power of God. The work here is to gain that blessing for your relationship as well as the relationships and children your usness produces.

One of our blessings in life has been to learn about this new tact of marital work over the last twenty years. First, from wise therapists like Shawn Stoever and Nathan Phillips. Second, from committed friends willing to do anything for couples to help them like Steve and Rajan Trafton. Third, through a group of insightful colleagues at Amarillo Family Institute who were willing to take everything we had learned, written about, and saw in therapy to hammer out a model that was both new and old at the same time and ended up being very helpful and beneficial to couples. Fourth, from colleagues, trainees, and students at Fuller Theological Seminary who were willing to learn the psychoeducational approach of RelateStrong and the therapeutic model of Restoration Therapy. Finally, through ordinary couples just like Ron and Nan Deal. They are the real heroes. The ones who were at the end of their ropes when their relationship had seemingly gone over the cliff and were holding on by a thread. The ones who were willing to look at themselves and face their own pains and came to the most interesting of conclusions—that indeed there was hope walking through the process of mindfulness to find not only peace in their relationship, but love, joy, patience, kindness, goodness, faithfulness, gentleness, and self-control. In the pages that follow, you will learn the story of Ron and Nan. They know how this process of taking off the old self and putting on the new can revolutionize everything not only about yourself but also about your usness. As you read, we pray you learn about your own strength to be kind, to be loving, and to be wise in how you love and live with your us every day and find joy in all God has given you through your marriage.

Introduction

Nan and I married in the middle of an Iowa snowstorm in January 1986—a tender moment in the middle of a severe weather threat. It was an ominous start to happily ever after. Nearly two decades later, Nan called me into our bedroom, sat me down, and said, "I can't live like this. One of us has to leave."

Our marriage looked pretty good from the outside. Nan worked as a teacher and focused her energies on our kids and home. I was a practicing marriage and family therapist, counseling couples and families in distress. Helping families thrive was my passion. So how was my own marriage imploding?

"I'll get us some help," I said.

"Today," she said. "We can't put this off anymore."

I tried reaching out to a few trusted counselors, yet nobody had an immediate opening.

"There's a leading theoretician in the field of psychotherapy who lives in our city," I told Nan. "But there's probably no way we can get in to see him. He has a six-month waiting list."

"Call him," she said. "Now."

Her tone was serious and colder than that snowstorm on our wedding day. By some miracle, Dr. Terry Hargrave made time for us, working us into his schedule the very next day.

"Who wants to go first?" he asked on that first visit.

"Me," Nan said. "But let's get one thing straight. You're both clinicians, so don't you dare gang up on me. No psychobabble, mumbo-jumbo. Just speak in layman's terms."

"Gladly," Terry said.

I agreed, too.

Nan explained to Dr. Hargrave how lonely she felt in our marriage. Neither of us had had an affair and there weren't outrageous vices that were glaring reasons for mistrust. Nan had simply grown weary of feeling like she played second fiddle to my work ministering to couples and families. Ironic, I know.

I had heard Nan's complaints before. In fact, she'd leveled her accusations and anger my way many times. But she didn't understand my heart. *I have a divine calling*, I thought. *How dare she stand in judgment when she's the needy one?*

After twenty minutes, Terry made a simple reflective statement to summarize Nan's experience. He was speaking to her, but I sensed he was talking to me. "So, what you're telling me, Nan, is the reason Ron threw you under the bus is because God told him to."

I was cut to the quick. Would God tell me to neglect my wife in selfish ambition? No way! Something was terribly wrong with how I had been treating her. Something had to change.

Over the next few sessions, Terry introduced us to Restoration Therapy (RT), a relatively new model of psychotherapy he had developed that combines attachment, emotional regulation, and mindfulness. Its pragmatic approach is based in theological principles and interpersonal neuroscience. With Terry and RT, Nan and I learned how we'd gotten to this crisis point—and, even better, how to avoid it in the future. We uncovered the why behind our pain. We learned to self-regulate. And we learned how to pivot from pain to peace.

Mindful | *adjective* | bearing in mind; attentive to; aware[1]

Being mindful involves fully attending to what you are feeling, what you do with those feelings, and the impact they have on your marital dance.

Dr. Hargrave is the architect of this highly acclaimed model used by thousands of clinicians worldwide. Sharon Hargrave, his wife, is a marriage and family therapist who helped develop RT and whose marital enrichment resources based on RT are used nationwide.[2] Nan and I benefited personally from their counsel and have shared RT with hundreds of satisfied couples. That's why we wrote this book. We want to make RT accessible to everyone without any mumbo-jumbo. No psychobabble. We aim to make it plain.

Until we tried Restoration Therapy, we struggled to find

peace in our marriage in spite of having access to the top-shelf marriage-enrichment books, tools, conferences, and Bible studies. I worked as a marital therapist and in ministry in local churches and with FamilyLife, a Christian non-profit. We had access to tremendous resources. And still we struggled in our marriage. Grief brought us together for a time when our twelve-year-old son, Connor, died, but the alliance was temporary. RT, however, helped us to restore peace, individually *and* as a couple.

So, we know firsthand that RT works. As Nan and I share these principles in seminars around the country, we hear things like, "Doors are opening that we didn't even know were shut." "Our relationship has grown by leaps and bounds!" We love sharing these life-giving principles. And we are honored to share them with you.

That snowy day in Iowa when Nan and I made our vows was romantic, but it couldn't hold a candle to the love we experience in our marriage today. This side of heaven, we will still experience unrest, insecurity, and pain. Knowing what to do when it comes has made all the difference. We're mindful now and living in peace. *And we want that for you, too.*

PART ONE

The Old Self

CHAPTER 1

Nurturing Your Usness

"Would you like to go to a concert tonight?"

I was shaving and Nan was drying her hair many years into our marriage when I asked her out on a date.

"That sounds nice," Nan said.

Wow! I thought. I smiled at her reflection in the bathroom mirror. I had conquered Mount Kilimanjaro, or so it felt. Finding activities to break up the monotony of life and add energy to our relationship had always been tricky. This win was a nice moment.

"Who else could we invite?" I asked.

Nan was hurt. I could see it immediately in her posture and in her eyes. *Wait, what did I say?* I wondered. And then came my typical thoughts to cope. *I never get anything right* (shame) and *What is her problem?* (blame and anger). Then, *Defend yourself, Ron!* (control).

Now, that was my perspective of that moment. Here's Nan's.

"Would you like to go to a concert tonight?"

Ron had just asked me out on a date. I'd been wanting time with him. He'd been preoccupied recently, bringing work home that distracted him. He'd arrived late and fell asleep early after giving his all at work. Now he wanted to spend time with me. I was so happy. Then he asked, "Who else could we invite?" *and I felt disappointment rush in.* He wants other people there, *I thought.* He's not focused on us at all. *I thought my loneliness had come to an end, but it hadn't.*

Wow. A peaceful moment turned into pain in the blink of an eye. I wanted to connect with Nan, and she wanted time with me. *How did we get here . . . again? Why can't we stop this cycle?*

We have since learned a term for what happened in that nanosecond: **emotional dysregulation**. Some call it getting triggered. Anxious. Freaking out. It's a neurological reality that occurs in every human being at some point—even multiple times a day. Emotional dysregulation is when the limbic system, particularly what is referred to as the midbrain or the "downstairs" brain, pumps the body full of energy when it perceives a threat, whether physical or emotional. This rudimentary part of the brain readies the body for action—for self-protection.

There's an antidote to this triggered feeling: **self-regulation**. In self-regulation we engage the thinking part of the brain—the prefrontal cortex or the "upstairs brain." That's the area responsible for decision-making, drawing conclusions, delaying gratification, and solving problems.

To put it simply, the midbrain *reacts*. The prefrontal cortex *considers*.

When the midbrain drives behavior, we're impulsive.

When the prefrontal cortex is engaged, we're deliberate. Self-controlled. Mindful. Self-regulation moves you away from reacting out of pain and moves you into responding out of thoughtful choice.

Every response we make matters. Why? Because behaviors eventually become habitual. Neurological pathways become set, creating patterns of dysregulation or regulation. In RT we call these pain and peace cycles.[2] Such cycles can be activated in a split second.

In a relationship, one person's reactivity often taps the pain center of the other partner. In other words, dysregulation in one partner invites dysregulation in the other. When I asked Nan to the concert, I felt calm and was moving toward her in love, engaging my upstairs brain. But when I *sensed* her disappointment, *my downstairs brain kicked in.*[3] I sensed a threat, and I became emotionally dysregulated and reactive. Neurologically speaking, *anxiety took my mind captive* and my pain cycle took over. Reacting with blame and controlling behavior triggers Nan's pain cycle, and she, too, began reacting.

In RT, Dr. Hargrave helped me map and sequence my personal patterns of reactivity. Nan mapped hers, too. We were then able to see how our individual pain cycles intersect and create a couple pain cycle. Mapping our pain cycles was absolutely life-changing. When we could identify what triggered us and how, we could learn how to self-regulate. We used to try to manage each other. Now we manage ourselves. That switch has made all the difference.

This book will help you learn what triggers you. You'll learn how to stop reacting and start being *mindful.* Mindfulness, for you, will look different from mine or Nan's because every individual's pain and peace cycles are unique. You bring your wiring into whatever relationships you're in. Learning to self-regulate when you're feeling dysregulated is key to cultivating a peaceful self, a peaceful marriage, and a peaceful life together.

BRAND-NEW

Nan and I happen to love Jesus. It's one thing that attracted us to each other. We live out love, kindness, and self-control like Jesus...some days. On others, it's extremely difficult to do so. Happily, RT helps us integrate what we believe the Bible teaches with what we've learned about human behavior and neuropsychology.

For example, the New Testament teaches that followers of Jesus are a "new creation" (2 Cor. 5:17 ESV). In him we already have salvation and hope, but we are still moving into our new self. By grace, we're forgiven and adopted into God's family and yet at times the old self still hijacks our mind, heart, and behavior.

The apostle Paul addressed this struggle, writing about the desire to do what is right but not being able to carry it out. Nan and I relate to that. Do you? "I want to do what is good, but I don't. I don't want to do what is wrong, but I do it anyway" (Rom. 7:19 NLT). That's the old self rearing its ugly head.

I desired to love Nan well, but my old self got in the way. When I sensed Nan's disappointment, I reacted in defensiveness and blame, even though I knew better and wanted more for us.

I needed a new mind. I was aware of the New Testament's challenge to us that we discipline our minds and be "transformed by the renewal of [the] mind" (Rom. 12:2 ESV). Renewal comes by setting the mind "on things above" and by putting "to death" the works of the flesh, growing in the fruits of the Spirit, including self-control (Col. 3:1–17 and Gal. 5:16–26). And what is the promised result? Peace. With a focus on truth (and things that are honorable, just, pure, lovely, admirable, of excellent character, or praiseworthy) and by putting truth into practice, *the God of peace will be with us* (Phil. 4:8–9).

Our marriage has crashed and burned more than once. Or maybe I should say our *old selves* crashed, reactively. By practicing RT, we've learned to mindfully choose attitudes and behaviors that foster peace. A new mind, renewed in Christ, chooses self-regulation over reactivity. That's what Restoration Therapy is all about: restoring peace.

The biblical language of a new mind and a new self may seem abstract. But modern science underscores its deeper wisdom borne out in modern neurological research. The emerging research around neuroplasticity reveals that the human brain is capable of tremendous growth and change, well into adulthood. The wisdom of scripture and modern medical science synthesize here in this good news: it's possible to actively participate in renewing our mind, taking off the dysregulated, reactive self and responding instead from the mind of Christ (powered by the prefrontal cortex). In a very real sense, our brain is being made new all the way down to its neural networks; indeed, *we* are being made new!

The gospel promise of renewal is true for us individually and it's true in our intimate relationships. Married couples easily see the contrast between the old and new self. Let's revisit the story at the beginning of this chapter. While I wish I had responded to Nan's concert disappointment with a "soft answer" (Prov. 15:1), my old, dysregulated self activated anger and control reactions. Nan, in her old self, became angry and critical when hurt. Then our negative interactions escalated quickly from there.

When triggered, responding in love and truth is tough. Nan and I needed to learn to self-regulate and mindfully choose peace.

FOCUS IN DYSREGULATED MOMENTS

The pride I felt in bringing my wife joy by asking her to the concert and finding something fun we could enjoy together turned to pain quickly when I sensed her hurt. My thoughts turned to *my* hurt, *my* worry that she might disapprove of me, and the pain of a strained relationship. My focus was on me. Me, me.

One of the things I've learned from RT is that when I feel my wife's disappointment, I try to control her to get her to approve of me again. Essentially, I focus on changing her to make my pain go away. It's as if I'm saying, "Something's wrong here and, honey, it's you. Let me change you with my anger and defensiveness." Essentially, this is going a thousand miles an hour down the Dysregulation Freeway, heading toward disaster, and saying, "I'm okay, you're not, so you have to change—and I have the right to make it happen."

That prideful posture calls for a reality check.

How do controlling and angry reactions impact others? Short answer: they hurt. They amplify dysregulation. Trying to change a person so they act in a way that eliminates your pain simply does not work. Instead, we can become mindful of our own thoughts and behaviors—and our dysregulation. That takes humility, which means, literally, *thinking rightly of oneself.* The Latin root word of "humility" is *humilitas*, meaning "grounded" or "from the earth." In other words, humility brings us down to earth. In *Learning Humility*, Richard Foster invites us to get grounded as it relates to God and others. "We don't think of ourselves higher than we should. Nor do we think of ourselves lower than we should. No pride or haughtiness. No self-depreciation or feelings of unworthiness. Just an accurate assessment of who we actually are."[4] Then, with my humility activated, I'm able to resist judgment of my spouse. I can take charge of myself. I consciously let go of that old self—the controlling me—and focus on what's true.

Humility shifts my focus away from my spouse to how I can regulate myself. It's akin to exiting the Dysregulation Freeway; it decreases anxiety (slowing the respiratory system, blood pressure, and heart rate). It's a healthier, more peaceful direction.* Humility is the moment-by-moment, day-to-day putting on of the new self. With humility, we can literally renew the mind. We'll show you a process to help you do just that.

NURTURING USNESS

Your usness, as the Hargraves like to call it, is who you are together. It's the third part of your relationship. There's you, your spouse, and your usness. Usness was born the day you married. It's made up of your promises, behaviors, and your mutual love. You sacrifice for it, long for it, and even panic when you think it's coming apart. It gives back, too. It looks out for the good of the relationship. It allows you as individuals to grow and benefit from the shelter it provides, and it makes you feel at home with each other. When usness is strong—when it is alive and bubbling over with intimacy—there is peace. When you are anxious about the condition of your usness, there is pain. Pain triggers dysregulation.

When two healthy individuals feed and nurture their usness, it will grow and remain strong over time. So, how does usness receive nurture? We'll talk about that in the next chapter. For now, know that self-regulation empowers your usness; it allows you to bring your best self to the

---

* If you are being abused emotionally, sexually, or physically, or if your partner is actively engaged in an addiction, don't hear us saying that by changing yourself you can change them. They need to take charge of their own behavior and make significant changes, and you need to seek safety. Reach out to a professional who can guide you along the way. See appendix 2.

relationship. And when both of you self-regulate, you can create a great us.

NEW SELF, PEACEFUL US CONVERSATION:

- Every one of us becomes emotionally dysregulated from time to time. Do you have a sense of when it happens in you?
- What part of the apostle Paul's struggle between his old self and his new self can you relate to?
- What is your reaction to this statement, "Humility is not thinking poorly of yourself or thinking yourself less valuable than another, it is thinking rightly about yourself"?
- When do you have a posture of pride toward your spouse focusing on things you think they need to change?
- What feels healthy about your usness? What are you concerned about?

CHAPTER 2

The Two Pillars of a Healthy Relationship: Love and Trust

Emotionally healthy adults have strong identities and feel safe in relationships. Identity comes by knowing you're loved, unique, worthy of receiving love, and that you belong. Feeling safe includes trusting your physical surroundings, including the provision of shelter and food, and having faith in relationships, that is, believing that your world and the important people in it are trustworthy, reliable, honest, transparent, and fair.

Love flourishes when identity and safety are secure. Conversely, when identity and safety are insecure, we feel pain—activating fight-or-flight reactivity. (Others add freeze, fawn and flop reactions. From a neurological perspective, we believe these additional expressions are rooted in fight or flight, e.g., freeze is an extreme form of flight. And while fawn and flop are reactions we have, they are more based on and influenced by our reasoning and habits. Fight and flight are automatic reactions and based in the midbrain. For more, see chapter 4.)

If I sense that I can trust you, I will feel safe and interact with you in a relaxed and loving way. This increases the likelihood that you will feel and respond in the same ways, which then increases our feelings of safety and trust in each other. Love and trust exist and work together to boost our identities and liberate us toward fun, sensuality, vulnerability, and a deep sense of partnership and companionship. *Love* tells me who I am; it shapes and informs my *identity*. *Trust* tells me that I am emotionally safe; it shapes and informs my sense of *safety* within my relational world.

All relationships (especially marriage) require love *and* trust for partners to experience worth and emotional safety. Indeed, it is the combination of the two that is so powerful and life-giving to us as individuals and to relationships.

Striving for this in earthly relationships is important. The fuel for doing so is the spiritual source of love and trustworthiness.

DIVINE LOVE

Human relationships require a mutual give and take. God's love and faithfulness do not. They are inviolable aspects of God's nature. "For the LORD is good; his steadfast love endures forever, and his faithfulness to all generations" (Ps.

100:5 ESV). His love is loyal and faithful. It is everlasting. When everything else is unsure, we can count on God.

God's loving and trustworthy nature is confirmed repeatedly in the Bible. Our identity is confirmed, too, since we are called God's beloved children, adopted sons and daughters, children of the King. That's our identity. The stability of our relationship with God is never in question because we are infinitely valuable to God (see Matt. 6:25–34) and he will never leave us nor forsake us (Heb. 13:5). Because of God's love and steadfast commitment, we can draw near with confidence and full assurance (Heb. 10:19–22).

God provides identity and safety in our relationship with him when we are in peaceful times and in difficult times. This truth fuels our ability to give and receive love and faithfulness to and from others.

Hypothetically, what if God wasn't faithful? What if God was unreliable? What if the scriptures read, "His love endures . . . as long as you do everything he says," or "as long as he feels like it"? And what if the purpose of God's love was to manipulate you into being what he wants you to be. There would be no emotional safety in a relationship with God. You would never know your standing before him. You would be anxious, fearful, and you would doubt the intent of his principles and boundaries for holy living.

These absurd questions illuminate the importance of emotional safety in relationships. Love without safety is unbearable.

God loves perfectly and is faithful forever. Humans do not and cannot. We do not live up to our intended love or trustworthiness. Yet God's perfect love and faithfulness can fuel and mature our imperfect love if we let it soak into our being.

WHAT IS TRUE ABOUT YOU AND YOUR IDENTITY

Here's what we know about your identity. God knit you together in your mother's womb (Ps. 139:13). Your uniqueness and worthiness were with you at birth and remain with you today. You are profoundly gifted, talented, and a masterpiece (Eph. 2:10). Your identity is bound inextricably with that of your Creator. No wonder he loves you so much—you're his! Though you may not always feel it, you are special and tremendously worthy.

Your identity isn't about your looks, your job, the car, the people you know or call friends, the number of followers you have on social media, or any other external thing about you. Your identity is that you are a beloved child of God. Your divinely given gifts, talents, and abilities are aspects of you that are creative and good. What you bring to your marriage is good. Do not miscalculate your worth as being bad or of little value. Humility, remember, is thinking rightly. God affirms you with a yes that you are loved, held, and precious.

Embracing your God-given identity can be tough when earthly relationships fall short. Dr. Hargrave confesses he struggles with this. He grew up in a physically and emotionally abusive home. "My siblings and I were always fed, clothed, and had a roof over our heads—but the lack of affirmation or expressions of love made me feel unloved, unwanted, and like I did not belong." Those challenges impacted him in ways he's still figuring out today, even years after years of personal and professional growth, including founding a movement that helped tens of thousands of people restore their God-given identity.

See? We are all a work in progress.

Mindfully hold these notions in tension: Each of us is precious in God's sight *and* flawed. You are loved exactly as you are and, yet, in God's kindness, he empowers you to grow.

It's time to grow. More specifically, it's time to grow beyond your pain.

THE QUESTIONS PAIN ASKS

Nan and I were reacting in pain in our conversation about the concert. Let's explore the questions pain asks about our identity and safety.

"Am I Loved?"

Your lived experiences create your personhood and your sense of self—this is your identity. The assurance that you're unique, worthy, and you belong result in the feeling of being well loved.

Infants are biologically wired to seek what they need *externally*. Babies, after all, have precious little personal agency. They depend on caregivers for their means of survival—nurture, protection, and guidance.

That's why babies are biologically wired with a primal drive to emotionally attach with the adults around them. This helps them attach to a caregiver (usually one or both parents). As psychiatrist Curt Thompson puts it, we're born into this world "looking for someone who is looking for us."[1]

An infant who is cuddled, cared for, attended to, and comforted by a nurturing presence bonds with that caregiver. Healthy parents respond with words and actions that say, "I see you. I know you. You're safe." This begins an attachment process that stimulates the infant's brain, affirming worth and safety.

So critical is attachment between newborn and caregiver that it must happen within the first twenty-four hours or that infant will be noticeably agitated and distressed. If bonding doesn't happen in the first seventy-two hours, distress intensifies. The baby will become less responsive and distracted, and take in less nutrition. If bonding doesn't happen within a week or so, the infant will manifest characteristics of Failure to Thrive syndrome—a condition that's fatal if untreated.

As we grow past infancy, we begin to understand our place in the world by understanding ourselves in relation to others. Our *identity* is the expression of our perceived sense of importance, and we learn who we are from the way that our most important caregivers love us.

When a child is celebrated, nurtured, and affirmed, they feel safe, protected, like they belong. Conversely, children who experience abuse, feel neglected, or don't sense their own worth have difficulty forming healthy identities. They may believe they lack worth or are unworthy of love. Identity formation has a deep and lasting impact.

It's important to note that other, nonparental relationships and traumatic experiences can also shape identity (and our sense of safety). Stepparents, teachers, coaches, neighbors, and peers play a part. We may feel special or average, included or rejected—loved or unloved—because of those relationships. Traumatic events bring lasting harm. Imagine, for example, how difficult it is to feel loved and unique in the midst of a war-torn country where food and shelter are sparse, and you could be killed at any moment. Or consider the impact sexual or physical abuse has on how someone thinks of themselves (identity). What if a family member were suddenly killed by an accident or murder (safety)? Just as healthy love is powerful in its ability to shape our senses of self for the good, unloving experiences can shape it for the bad.

"Am I Safe?"

Contrary to popular belief, love is not all we need. If your partner says they love you, for example, but they repeatedly bring you harm, you will not flourish. We need to be able to trust our world and find emotional safety in our most intimate relationships. This is the second pillar to healthy relationships. Your brain not only comes equipped with a program to bond and attach to someone who will love you, it also has a program to read the environment to determine whether or not any given situation is safe to interact in. When the environment is unsafe or relationships feel threatening, we take protective or aggressive action. We commonly call these *fight-or-flight reactions.*

In a mutually loving relationship that we can trust to be emotionally safe most of the time, we experience peace. Creativity, innovation, and growth flourish. Partners in such an environment feel free to enjoy their work, give to their community out of a sense of abundance, even take risks as they love, honor, and cherish one another. Emotional safety helps each partner to gladly make sacrifices for the other, and be quick to cooperate, negotiate, and communicate with openness and deep attunement. Partners in safe relationships have fun together, are quick to forgive, and give each other the benefit of the doubt when minor irritations occur.

Nan and I have experienced lots of these beautiful moments. They tend to make painful interactions more confusing. We wonder, *Why are we so good together much of the time, then so bad together at other times?* We really do desire each other. When our usness is in a state of peace, desire easily flows out of us in loving and trustworthy ways. But when in pain, unmet desires for identity and safety are expressed in unloving and untrustworthy ways. That, in turn, increases perceived threat and decreases safety between us—it's a vicious cycle.

Have you ever gone to a marriage seminar and learned skills that had a positive impact on your marriage, only to discover you're unable to use those skills during an argument? This is why. When regulated (in peace) the brain easily accesses and utilizes these valuable skills, but when dysregulated (in pain, feeling unloved or unsafe), the thinking brain isn't working and skills we possess go out the window.

One more thought: Just as *identity* in intimate relationships is based on attachment and childhood experiences, our sense of *safety* forms in the context of early family experiences, stressful adult relationships, and/or traumatic experiences. Both identity and safety get expressed in adulthood.

Trust depends on three essential factors

1. **Reliability.** When I take my dog to the groomer, I expect to return to find her clean and happy. If not, I will stop using that groomer because *I do not trust them to do what they say.* If, however, the groomer does a good job, I'll keep going back. I trust them. If my dog isn't cleaned and ready once in a great while, I will likely continue to give them my business because even though they are not perfect they're consistent. The same is true in personal relationships. If we can predict loving and reliable interactions, we can tolerate occasional disappointment. However, when someone is reliable less than 90 percent of the time, we hesitate to trust.

2. **Transparency.** Transparency cultivates trust. Secrets undermine trust. Have you ever experienced relationships or situations where secrets were kept, or someone was unwilling to be open or honest with you? Perhaps in school a group of people excluded you from knowing something, keeping you on the outside. Perhaps a member of your family acted strangely with no explanation. You knew something was wrong, but you didn't know what. It is simply impossible to feel safe in relationships

when we do not have the whole story and truth. At best, we will withdraw and be tentative in the relationship; at worst, we'll cut ties altogether.

3. **Fairness.** Healthy relationships depend on mutual give-and-take. This is true in business relationships, friendships, and diplomacy between countries. And in well-defined relationships like family and marriage, we expect to receive expressions of love even as the other expects to receive them from us. In high-risk relationships like marriage this sense of fairness is essential. I give Nan love as expressed in my heart, sexual fidelity, time, dedication to her care and provision, and financial resources, and, in fairness, I expect the same from her. It does not have to be an exact 1:1 give-and-take situation, and no one is earning points, keeping a ledger to win the other's obligation, or seeking to gain an advantage in the relationship. But neither can we expect to be vulnerable with each other if love and trust is not reciprocated.[2]

Seasons of imbalance in fairness can challenge trust. While I was in graduate school, Nan worked three jobs and took care of our home. I didn't contribute much to our household, and I didn't have much time for her. Over time that disproportionate investment of time and energy balanced out between us—but for a while it was a strain. Other couples experience periods in health or education or caregiving where one partner contributes more to the relationship—and that's OK. The issue is not whether the ledger is equally balanced at any given moment;

Strong & Healthy Relationships

L o v e

—Unique

—Worthy

—Belonging (Not alone)

Reliability—

Transparency— (Openness)

Fairness—

T r u s t

Identity ("Who am I?")

Safety ("Am I safe?")

Two Pillars of a Healthy Relationship

the issue of safety is instead an outcome of fairness and justice over time.

PRIMED FOR LOVE AND SAFETY

When we know our worth as God's children and receive consistent love from our family of origin (childhood), we are primed for adult relationships including marriage and parenting. We know what it is to receive love, and we understand how to be a trustworthy presence in the life of someone we care about. In marriage, trust and emotional safety results in each partner giving abundantly of themselves to the other. We do not wait for the other to give before we give in return—we give freely *first* because we *trust* the other will always give freely also.

A secure identity in God's love and faithfulness fuels loving and trustworthy actions that build, nourish, and sustain healthy relationships. In a mutually loving, trusting relationship, we love freely, usness matures, and the individuals thrive. The giving and the receiving create a cycle of peace that never ends, till death do us part.

However, it takes only a nanosecond for unloving or unsafe actions to create pain, and for pain to threaten peace. *Every* partner struggles with pain. In the next chapter we'll examine your pain, the story it tells, and how it impacts your marriage.

NEW SELF, PEACEFUL US CONVERSATION:

- What does God's steadfast and faithful love tell you about your worth, identity, and eternal safety? (If you're not sure this is true about you, how might you feel if it was?)
- If you could lean into the truth about yourself from God's point of view, how would that make a difference when you don't feel loved or safe with your spouse?
- Review the illustration on page 23 about the Two Pillars of Healthy Relationships. Notice the descriptive

words (e.g., Unique, Transparency, etc.). What would it look like to have them in your marriage often?

- If you feel safe enough, share your responses to the following questions with your spouse:

  How did you know (as a child) you were loved?

  How did you know you were safe?

  What did you have to do (as a child) to make sure things were safe?

  At times when you didn't feel loved or safe, what did these moments say about your worth or value or tell you about how to behave?

CHAPTER 3

What's My Trigger?
My Pain Story

It's human to feel pain.

Theft, lies, and deceit hurt deeply. Maybe that's your story. Or maybe you were exploited sexually. Maybe you've been manipulated. Neglected. Abused. In pain, you might have withdrawn and stayed emotionally on guard or become aggressive and defensive. Blame, shame, control, escape— and any combination of the four—are common reactions. And pain from the past can keep us from being vulnerable in the present, even in emotionally safe relationships.

We've all experienced pain. What matters here is not so much the injury itself but the story pain taught us about ourselves, the world, and relationships. (If you have been deeply hurt by something your spouse or someone else did, this next part may be difficult to process, but stay with us.)

Someone's pain story is often recounted as moments or events that damaged trust or made them feel unwanted or

unloved. "My dad was never around. I guess we didn't matter that much to him." "My mom's phone is her first love."
"I got her coffee, but all she could do was complain that it
was too cold." Or "Everything and everyone seems more
important to him than me." For some, the moments are
physically violent, sexually manipulative, or emotionally
abusive. These circumstances should not be minimized and
need the guidance of someone outside your marriage, pref-
erably a professional therapist. (If this is you, please pause
and read appendix 2.)

As hurtful as these situations are—and many of them
are traumatic in their own right—the ultimate source of
the pain you carry is not any one relationship or instance.
Rather, the source of your pain—and what generally steals
peace—is a cumulative story your brain has put together
over time. This story is written often from a series of painful situations or relationships and your interpretation of
what those relationships say about you. Most specifically,
the story centers on your perceived sense of worthiness to
be loved (identity) and whether you are safe in relationships
(whether people and relationships can be trusted).

This story is so powerful that when negative things happen—
whether minor irritations or significant difficulties—the story
that immediately pops into our heads is the one we have
been telling ourselves, sometimes for a very long time. The
story is complex and written in a muddled and often ran-
dom way, but it has resulted in a particular set of feelings
about your identity and sense of safety to which you are
quite hypersensitive. So sensitive is your story, in fact, that
the least impingement or violation to these feelings reminds

you of the whole ball of entangled thoughts, emotions, and meaning of your life's interactions with pain. This activates your midbrain coping reactions, which are also entangled in your story of pain.

Have you ever reacted to your partner's behavior or words in a way that was out of line with what they were really saying? Your reaction was a 9 on a 10 scale, but it turned out their words were a 2. Something in their words triggered *your* pain story.

For example, the cumulative story your brain tells may be that relationships and people can't be trusted. When you start to suspect your spouse is keeping a secret, you may immediately suspect he's having an affair and that he isn't committed to you—then you blow up and accuse him of betraying you. Later you discover the truth: he's quietly planning a surprise party for your birthday. Your story of pain doesn't discriminate objectively; it simply reacts, often in self-destructive ways.

Consider another example. Margie didn't grow up feeling safe with her mother. In fact, she frequently felt abandoned by her throughout her life. Still, she made weekly calls to check on her mom. In one such call, her mother talked about the weather, her parakeet, and the neighbor's stolen lawn mower, followed by a quick "Thanks for calling." Then she hung up. She didn't ask Margie about her life or well-being. Afterward, Margie felt muddled. She had thoughts of resentment, and longing, wondering why she wasn't worth her mother's time or attention. Later, when she dropped her coffee mug, coffee splashed on her white jeans and she said, "I'm such a stupid klutz!" Objectively we can see that this circumstance is about Margie's mom and her inability to love and take interest in her daughter. But the cumulative story in Margie's brain is one of shame. She blames herself for her mother's lack of love—she must have done something wrong, or she'd surely receive her mother's attention. Margie's story of pain drives her reactivity. Oh, and it doesn't just stop there. Margie's shame extends to her marriage. She regularly hears criticism from her husband when he doesn't intend it and blames herself when he is inattentive. Her brain makes sense of the world through the lens of that pain no matter the relationship, past or present.

TRIGGERED

Your hidden story of pain that shapes your sense of identity and safety is why you occasionally feel triggered. This may happen when you are processing even an innocuous comment. If the comment has any correlation with a past pain, your brain and body will react. Note that your entire body reacts as well. When you are reminded of your story of pain, your sympathetic nervous system (SNS) mobilizes every function of your body (heart rate, respiratory rate, blood pressure, etc.) to support self-preserving, fight-or-flight behaviors. An emotional can of worms may open up inside. You may feel upset and dysregulated before you can even think, and you immediately become reactive.

But why does our story of pain take over? Millions of neurons in the brain fire to produce your thoughts and actions. When thoughts or actions are repeated, you fire the same sequence of neurons. What's known as Hebbian theory, or "assembly theory," teaches us the neurons that fire together, wire together. This means that repetitive thoughts or actions statistically increase the tendency of those neurons to fire again in that sequence. And since familiar neuronal sequence firing is more efficient, your brain actually comes to prefer that neuronal sequence and will activate it instantly. That's why your pain story triggers dysregulation of mind, body, and soul even when logically it shouldn't. At that point, a pain story that originated in your past suddenly emerges in the present and prompts the meaning you ascribe to your circumstances and how you react.

Take sibling rivalry, for example. Many children suspect that they were not as loved by their parents as a sibling, or that a younger sibling displaced them within the family. Their identity is shaped as unloved and unimportant in that context. As an adult, that child may feel insecure in their marriage and struggle with feelings of unimportance to their spouse. It's annoying when a spouse responds to a ding on their phone in the middle of a conversation. But to a person hypersensitive to feeling unimportant, this act of phubbing (phone partner snubbing) becomes proof of their unimportance and a reason for distrust and distance. The cumulative story of pain hijacked the narrative of the moment, adding further damage to the person's sense of identity and safety. And, as you'll see, their reactivity will undoubtedly make things worse in the relationship.

We all carry a story of pain. Can you articulate yours? In

the next chapter we will explore what we typically do with our pain, but for now we want to invite you to face your story of pain. It's difficult to put words on these negative experiences. But here's what you need to know. It controls you whether you recognize it or not. Your old self is neurological; the pathways of pain and reactivity are set, which is why you keep *doing the things you do not want to do*. You can change what you notice. You can't change what you don't name.

Nan and I had to learn this the hard way. Remember that moment in Terry's office (told in the Introduction) when I realized for the first time how prideful I had been to pursue my career at the cost of my wife and marriage? After that session, Nan and I began to explore our stories of pain and how they impacted our marriage. We identified our **individual pain cycles** and our **couple pain cycle**. We learned to operationalize a change process mentioned repeatedly throughout the New Testament (adopting the humility of Christ, taking off our old selves, and putting on the new). I learned that my "perfect family" wasn't so perfect after all, and Nan did some extensive family-of-origin work that continues to this day. In fact, everything we learned through RT continues to this day.

We all carry a story of pain. But some of us, like me, aren't in touch with it. Or maybe we can articulate the hurt but don't recognize how it contributes to our reactions today. Becoming more mindful in part means becoming intimately familiar with yourself and your pain story. Putting words on it is the first step. That's how you begin managing yourself and creating your best relationship.

Identifying Emotions in Your Pain Cycle

1. When I am triggered, how do I usually feel? When I am upset, what messages have I received about my worth, value, or importance from my spouse, family, or friends when I'm upset, and what emotions are connected to them?

Circle one or two emotions that best answer the question. If you circle more than two, put a star beside the emotions that are most common.

Unloved	Unworthy	Insignificant	Alone	Hopeless
Worthless	Devalued	Defective	Inadequate	Unappreciated
Rejected	Unaccepted	Unwanted	Abandoned	

Other: _____

The words you have circled usually pertain to the primary emotions associated with your IDENTITY when you are not feeling at peace.

2. When I am upset or unsettled, how do I usually feel about the situation or relationship? What messages about relationships have I received from family or friends, and what emotions are tied to them?

Circle one or two words that best describe how you feel.

Unsafe	Unfair	Used	Guilty	Unsure
Fearful	Powerless	Controlled	Out of Control	Unknown
Vulnerable	Disconnected	Betrayed	Insecure	Not Enough

Other: _____

The words you have circled almost always pertain to the primary emotions associated with your sense of SAFETY when you are not feeling at peace.

This is both a book and, in a way, a workbook. There are a few exercises throughout that we strongly encourage you to complete before continuing. The exercises provide helpful insights and culminate in a plan that will bring about renewal in your mind and strength to your usness. They take just a few minutes and build on each other, so pause for each one. *Remember, what you take out of this book is directly tied to the work that you put into these exercises.*

Start becoming familiar with your pain story by completing exercise 1 before continuing to read.

(NOTE: If you and your spouse are reading this book together, a second set of exercises are provided in appendix 3. If viewing each other's answers feels unsafe at this point in your relationship, please consider getting a second copy of the book.)

MY STORY OF PAIN

What you have just begun to do is articulate your story of pain so you do not have to continue to be a victim of it. When you have felt unloved, your brain created a story about your identity (worth or value) that you continue to tell yourself when you get upset. And when you haven't felt entirely safe in a relationship or circumstance, your mind also created a story about your vulnerability that you repeat whenever you find yourself in a similar situation. All this impacts your reaction and what you do in response to these circumstances (what you'll discover in the next chapter).

If you're like me, you found this exercise very difficult to do. I believed I always felt loved as a child, and no one in my family ever made me feel unsafe. Ever. Well, that was what I told other people and myself for a long time. But then I began to realize the story I was telling was in part a symptom of the pressure I was under as a child. "Make the family look good," I learned. "Act right so others will draw closer to Jesus," my evangelistic father communicated to me. As well-intentioned as they were, my parents did have high expectations for my behavior as a kid. I never wanted to disappoint them, so I kept the rules, skewed the truth to make me look good when I didn't, and performed to the top of my game as much as I could.

No, I wasn't abused in any way imaginable. But I had pain. And I carried that pain straight into my marriage— and my performance mentality created pain in my wife. But I was too busy performing to notice.

The point is this: Trust that the steps in this book hold great promise to mature you beyond what you can imagine. Even if it feels unnecessary, go through the process and see where it leads. I can tell you we won't leave you in your pain. In the following chapters we'll help you make sense of your pain story and your reactive behaviors. We'll also help you learn how to take off this old self and put on the new self. As your mindfulness grows, your marriage and your usness will, too.

NEW SELF, PEACEFUL US CONVERSATION:

- The origins of these painful emotions reside in both past and current relationships. At this point in your life, what is usually happening when you feel these strong, painful emotions? Talk aloud about a recent moment when you felt this pain. Saying it aloud won't resolve it (that part comes later), but it verbally acknowledges a part of you that is caught in your old self.

- Have you ever reacted to your partner's behavior or words in a way that was out of line with what they were really doing or saying? Which painful emotion were you feeling at the time?
- Our bodies carry our pain and trauma. Some experience it in their back/neck, stomach, gut, or head (headaches). What happens in your body when you feel pain (dysregulated)?
- This and the previous chapter may have resurrected some very difficult emotions. Begin journaling about these emotions as you continue reading. This may help you better understand your pain cycle.

Four Coping Reactions to Pain: Blame, Shame, Control, Escape

Triggered in a nanosecond on that morning I asked Nan on a date, my dysregulated emotions felt complex, scary, and overwhelming. We've since learned through RT that people react in four distinct coping categories: blame, shame, control, and escape. When we do not feel safe, neurological alarms activate in the body. Safety is primary. So, no matter whether a perceived threat feels severe, like a hostile animal attack, or mild, like an irritated spouse, the body reacts to restore safety.

Here's the problem: the impulse to restore safety using the four coping strategies often sabotage it. Yeah, that's ironic. The reactive behavior in a pain cycle usually makes things worse, not better. But before we dive in to explore this, we just want to pause and recognize the pain you identified in the last chapter. It might have been very heavy. You might have discovered that your "complaint" about your spouse isn't so much about them as it is about your painful history. You may be feeling overwhelmed. Maybe you're familiar with your pain story and are surprised at how pervasive lingering emotions are. Or maybe you've never connected your pain to your identity or sense of safety—and that raises new questions. Don't rush this. What you uncovered is what most people keep hidden their entire lives. Indeed, many adults spend their lives stuck in their pain stories.

I remember when I began my journey of understanding my story of pain (and I'm not finished, by the way). I felt overwhelmed. Befuddled. Angry. And frequently lost. The closer I got to my own story the more I realized just how enslaved I had been to it. Which may be one reason you are considering putting this book down. Hey look, pain is painful! But here's what Nan and I have learned: While uncomfortable, leaning into your story of pain is an act of trust in the God who sees your pain far better than you. It helps you understand how your old self reacts so that you can, as the Bible says, take it off. You can't put on the new self until you take off the dysfunctional one that has permeated every aspect of your mind, body, soul—and relationships.

In humility, become intimately familiar with your pain and how it controls you. And you'll need humility to directly combat the pride you have—that you don't know you have—about what you are due because of your pain.

Have you realized yet that this book is not about helping you change your spouse? It's about helping you change yourself. When diagnosing our marital spats or battles, most of us blame our spouses. Oh, of course, we know that we have some responsibility in problems, but we judge our-selves far less harshly than we judge our spouse. We judge ourselves on our motives and our spouse on their actions. *I know I was rude, but that's because you are ungrateful for the nice things I was trying to do for you.* Funny how that math always adds up in our favor. But the biggest reason we're kinder to ourselves is because we know how much love and desire we have for our spouse—and how much peace we want in our usness. And what we're usually reacting to is a sense that our spouse doesn't love and cherish us as much as we'd like. We want them to want us more than they seem-ingly do. And this apparent lack of want (desire) makes us feel unsafe. You see, we judge ourselves on our desire for the person and relationship, but we judge them on their actions that, to us, indicate a lack of love or desire for us. This lopsided perspective lets us feel that what we're doing and why we're doing it is admirable, faithful, decent, and loving—but it isn't. *I'm good; you're bad. I'm loving; you're selfish. I'm safe to be around; being with you makes me feel threatened. Essentially, I'm okay, and you're not. And that's not as it should be, so I have the right to change you.* That's pride!

Later in the book we're going to show you an important spiritual truth about how a posture of pride invites negativ-ity into usness, but for now let's focus on what we do with our pain and pride within marriage. This, too, has a pre-dictable shape to it. As you'll see, you have a set pattern of reactivity that more than likely prevents you from getting what you're hoping for.

EMOTIONAL DYSREGULATION AND THE PAIN CYCLE

Think of a time when you felt generally safe and loved in life. For some, that's almost every hour of every day; for others it's a rare experience that hasn't happened often enough. In those shining moments we know who we are and feel confident in being loved and held precious, unique, and important. Empowered by our gifts and talents, we interact with the world in positive and constructive ways. We bring our best self to the world with purpose, living in alignment with God's plan. Being regulated in your identity and sense of safety frees you to be loving and trustworthy. Totally fulfilled, able to give and receive love and safety.

In scripture, the word that best captures this expression of your best self is "shalom," which means "peace." But when you are not at peace, when pain enters your spirit, your old self reacts in ways that bring more pain. The irony is—and it is very important that you come to see this—that though you are trying to restore peace (in yourself and the relationship), your unchecked reactions bring more pain to you, to your usness, and to your partner.

Let's pick up our conversation about your story of pain and how the brain reacts to perceived threat (see chapter 1). The midbrain manages automatic functions like basic processing of memory, emotions, heart rate, blood pressure, breathing, and digestion. It is largely unconscious, keeping your body functioning without any conscious thought from you. When you experience some kind of threat, the mid-brain exists to keep you safe. It prepares you to react.

A number of years ago, I was hiking with my family through the Palo Duro Canyon in the Texas panhandle. I heard the distinct sound of a rattlesnake inches away. In a millisecond my midbrain activated every system in my body toward safety—and the safety of my children. I was mobilized in a split second to react with a *fight* response against the snake or *flight* response to escape. In the face of threat, the midbrain takes over and the prefrontal cortex—the thinking/processing part of your brain—gets pushed aside. The midbrain does not distinguish nuance. It doesn't distinguish between a rattlesnake, a car veering toward you, spilled hot coffee, your father's disappointment, or your spouse's criticism. They all register as threats to your identity and safety, and your brain and body jump into fight-or-flight reactions.

These automatic system responses are forms of *coping*. When threatened physically, your coping reactions may save your life, but in marriage coping isn't always positive. Keep in mind that the actions you take to mitigate painful feelings and restore peace often make things worse. The good news is that these reactions are predictable neurological ruts of your individual pain cycle. Once you sequence your pain cycle, you'll know what it is and why you keep on doing things you don't want to do. In RT we refer to this as "mapping a pain cycle." Instead of reacting in painful moments, you can learn to mindfully choose how to respond. You don't have to stay stuck. You can self-regulate. Become familiar with your pain cycle, and you can change it.

The table below shows four coping behaviors we deploy when we're dysregulated.

Which one characterizes how you tend to react when unsettled or anxious?

Fight *(External Energy)*	*Flight* *(Internal Energy)*
Blame	Shame
Control	Escape

Note that *blame* and *control* are externally focused, aggressive, fight reactions. *Shame* and *escape* are internal, flight reactions. All four attempt to alleviate pain in various ways. Imagine that rattlesnake on your path. Are you likely to be aggressive or fleeing in that scenario? Now imagine a critical comment from a family member. Which behavior would you engage then?

Keep in mind that your reactive behavior is trying to restore love and/or safety to your relationship. To do so, your highly efficient brain relies on the same tricks that it has used in the past. It's common to employ one, two, three, or even all four of these coping behaviors at one time.

In the following scenarios, see if you can pinpoint the **behavioral reactivity** or the actions taken to restore love or safety. Then identify the coping category or dysregulation—shame, blame, control, or escape.

A. *"I cannot live in a disorganized and chaotic house. It confuses my thinking and bothers me. So, I take control and tell you what needs to be done to make things okay for me. My needs justify this."*

B. *"I could not take my boss telling me about one more problem or being dissatisfied with my performance, so I just blew up, cussed at him, and quit my job!"*

C. *"Talking about serious issues is too much for me. Life is way too short to concentrate on problems that can't be solved. I just prefer to hang loose, have a few drinks, have fun, and not talk about heavy things."*

D. *"I know my friend wants me to be more open, but it does not come naturally to me. I think I was just born under a cloud. I'm not really worthy or deserving of anyone's friendship."*

In the above scenarios, each person felt a threat to their sense of identity (worth or feeling loved) and sense of safety, then took action (coping) to try and rectify the negative feeling. Here are the answers:

A. Behavioral Reactivity: taking control of the situation, telling others what to do. Coping Category: Control.

B. Behavioral Reactivity: verbally blowing up, being contemptuous toward someone, and quitting their job. Coping Categories: Blame and Escape.

C. Behavioral Reactivity: eat, drink, and be merry. Coping Category: Escape.

D. Behavioral Reactivity: withdrawn, reserved, insecure. Coping Category: Shame.

We all do at least one of these coping mechanisms. *All of us.* When our identity or safety feels threatened, we will take action in some way. Knowing our old self tendencies helps us avoid unhealthy coping.

Below are descriptions of each coping strategy. Pay special attention to your responses to each, and see if you are prone to do any of them.

BLAME

A person who feels unloved and/or unsafe may feel others are responsible. Common blamer behaviors are accusing, being angry, raging, being sarcastic, acting arrogant, being aggressive, threatening, retaliatory, and punishing. It is important to distinguish that what matters here is not that the blamer *feels* angry as much as he or she *reacts* with anger. Anger is the blamer's attempt to restore identity and safety. The blamer *feels* unsafe and/or unloved, so demanding or demeaning is an effort to regain love or safety.

Blame is unlikely to foster loving feelings in others. But remember, the sympathetic nervous system is not rational or thinking long-term; its singular focus is survival.

Blaming behaviors in relationships erode trust and safety. Aggressive forms of blame, such as threats, rage, and violence, *violate* others' sense of identity and safety. (How ironic that a person reacts with blame and anger because they feel unloved or unsafe, yet their own reactivity makes others feel unloved and unsafe.) And when blamers realize the damage they're causing, it can further intensify their own pain. It's a toxic cycle.

SHAME

Shame is another coping behavior option. When a shamer feels unsafe or unloved, they believe they deserve it. They blame themselves and beat themselves up for flaws real or imagined and believe they're undeserving as they are. They may engage in relentless critique, self-loathing, and even self-hatred.

In addition, shamers often seem depressed, negative, hopeless, and inconsolable. It's as if the shamer has a hole inside that simply cannot be filled. They may complain that they are not loved and may become manipulative, sulky, or even self-harming. It can be frustrating to try to love a shamer as they have difficulty receiving love. It is important to remember that they are not simply feeling sorry for themselves any more than a blamer is an evil or a vindictive person. People who react with shame feel deep pain; their method of flight from that pain is to blame themselves and put themselves down.

CONTROL

We all want to believe that we are competent and capable. The problem is, of course, that almost none of us are all that capable on our own. Only God is. Only God is truly in control. Once we are reminded of that truth, let's remember that we do not often make wise decisions on our own. But, while it is not wrong to do our best or to strive for excellence and higher competency, there is something insidious about trying to control things and have our own way.

A dysregulated person in pain may attempt to minimize hurt or more pain through control. It's a form of fight. Controllers are often performance driven and perfectionistic. They do not take input from others well and often react defensively when their performance is questioned. In relationships, they may come across as judgmental or critical, and they often engage in nagging or lecturing behaviors. In short, a person who is reactive by controlling seldom believes that he or she is wrong and has difficulty letting other people make decisions or contribute to the relationship in their own manner (e.g., through style, or according to their personality).

ESCAPE

Escape is a coping behavior resulting from feeling overwhelmed by circumstances or feelings. To escape pain, they disappear. They may physically disappear by retreating to another setting, an activity, or a solitary place. Or they may disappear emotionally by disconnecting from important relationships, checking out emotionally, or even disassociating cognitively from reality. Escapers may retreat into food or a substance or an activity (like screens, gambling, or porn) or become impulsive, dramatic, avoidant, or secretive. Such behavior makes a person seem less reliable and responsible to friends, family, or coworkers, which brings more pain and chaos. Thus, the cycle continues.

Escapers usually have deep feelings about safety, particularly when it comes to their abilities to take initiative, act in their own best interests, or feel empowered in an unsafe situation. Escape is often associated with trauma from sexual abuse, war, victimization, natural disasters, or domestic violence.

Do you recognize yourself in these coping categories? As previously said, you can be reactive in one, two, or even all four. Once you discover your coping methods, you can map your *pattern* of pain-coping reactivity. We call it your pain cycle. That's next.

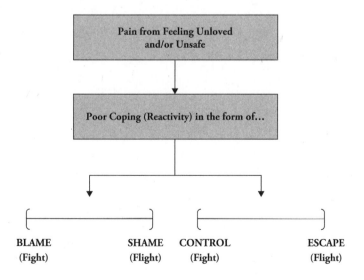

Various expressions of each:

BLAME	SHAME	CONTROL	ESCAPE
Blames Others	Shames Self	Controls	Escapes/Creates Chaos
Rage	Depressed	Perfectionistic	Impulsive
Angry	Negative	Performs	Numbs Out
Sarcastic	Whines	Judgmental	Avoids Issues
Arrogant	Inconsolable	Demanding	Escapes Using Substance
Aggressive	Catastrophizing	Critical	Escapes Using Activity
Retaliatory	Manipulative	Defensive	Irresponsible
Threatening	Fearful	Anxious	Selfish
Punishing	Pouting	Intellectualizes	Minimizes
Fault Finding	Harms Self	Nagging	Addicted
Discouraging	Needy	Lecturing	Secretive

NEW SELF, PEACEFUL US CONVERSATION:

- Why do we avoid exploring our pain story?
- People generally judge themselves based on their intentions and desire for the relationship but judge their partner based on what they do. In what way is this true for you?
- Every person has a neurological rut composed of a painful emotion that sparks predictable behavioral reactivity. What are you learning about how this works in your life?
- Which of the four reactions to pain (blame, shame, control, or escape) do you suspect you utilize most? Tell a story aloud of a recent time you acted in blame, shame, control, and/or escape.

CHAPTER 5

Mapping Your Pain Cycle

The date-night conversation that triggered Nan and me came on so fast. If only we could have hit Pause and slowed it all down. Then we might've made kinder, better choices that nurtured our usness. But both of us were in a rut—a neurological rut. My dysregulation invited Nan's and hers invited mine until we were again stuck in a painful cycle. What we've since learned is that pause *is* possible. It's possible with God's help and a humble heart to self-regulate your dysregulation. You can interrupt your neurological ruts with deliberate mindfulness.

To give your marriage a chance to grow, start with yourself. You can change something if—and only if—you recognize a need for growth and then identify the change that is needed.

Everyone has a pain cycle. You do, and your spouse does.

But yours is the one you can do something about.* There is no progress in pretending you do not have any areas that need change or in excusing them because you consider them less harmful than your spouse's. As Christians, our lifelong work is to continually refine our ability to take off our old self and put on a new self that increasingly looks like Jesus. Naming your pain cycle empowers you to change.

Nan and I have done, and *are still doing*, the same work, so we are sharing our pain cycles to illustrate how what we've discussed so far has benefited us.

RON'S PAIN CYCLE: THE CONTROLLER-PERFORMER

I grew up in a home with parents who loved the Lord, each other, and the four of us kids (three sons and a daughter). I consider myself one of the "blessed ones" because my parents valued kindness, honesty, and serving one another and those around them. My home was fun-loving, filled with joy, and safe. But of course, my family was not perfect. There was a dynamic in my home that led me to believe that merit or performance made a person valuable. As domestic and foreign missionaries, my parents took advantage of

---

* Abusive or destructive behavior is never acceptable. Demeaning or abusive behaviors or attitudes are not okay. If you're in an abusive relationship, seek outside help immediately. It's impossible to make a spouse kind, loving, and compassionate. You do not have that much control. We are simply inviting you to focus on what you bring to the marriage and grow by the Spirit of God. Let your spouse focus on changing themselves. See appendix 2 for more.

every opportunity to influence people toward Christ. They expected the whole family to help. A repeated nonverbal message throughout my childhood was *Act right so others will see Jesus*. Another was *Don't misbehave because that will hurt our ability to influence others*. I felt a lot of pressure to perform, not disappoint my parents, and make the family look good. I toed the line as a child, but disapproval and failure, it seemed, were always one mistake away.

I never felt unloved, but I was afraid that I would not be enough or measure up, or that I would reflect badly on my father and somehow lose his love. I performed. As long as I did, I felt competent in life and adequate, safe, and clear in my identity. Failure to perform meant failure as a son and as a person. This dynamic shaped my sense of identity and safety. My identity was tied to my performance in life; therefore, emotional safety in relationships felt fragile—just one mistake and I could lose everything.

In addition to all this, I come from a family of controlling performers—individuals who like it the way they like it and believe their way is best—and aren't afraid of telling you that. My grandmother was one of these controlling performers. As her only child, my father learned to be a controlling performer. Later I, too, became a performer, in effect placing my worth (identity) in the hands of others. I strove to meet and exceed the expectations of family members, friends, girlfriends, professors, customers—of everyone, especially employers and those who meant the most to me. I didn't just want their approval; I wanted to impress. And so, I performed and performed and performed.

Nan's opinion of me has always been at the top of my

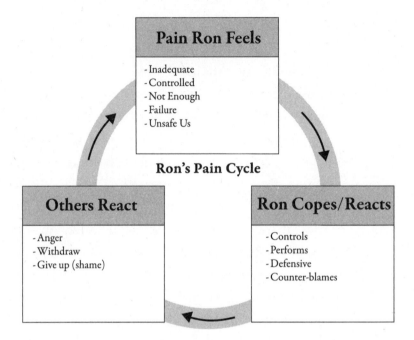

Illustration 1: Ron's Pain Cycle

list. When I feel her approval is at risk, when she is angry or displeased, that triggers my control reactions so I can cope with pain (disapproval) by trying to restore safety (approval and affirmation). At best her disapproval brings a slight tension to our relationship that I want to remove; I want us to be jovial, engaging, and happy to be with each other. At worst, I intuit from Nan's disapproval that my performance was lacking, I'm a failure, and that our relationship is in jeopardy. I react by immediately going to work to prove her wrong, change her perspective, and push away the blame (often back on her).

My control-performing behavior often comes across as reasonable (at least to me) and "intelligent," which I used against

Nan when I didn't feel enough approval from her. Let me explain. My parents were affectionate and worked well together. They lived with integrity and faithfulness. When they had conflicts, however, they would calmly retreat outside of our hearing to work it out. I never saw how they resolved conflict, I just knew my mom won a little and my dad won a lot. As a result, I had no experience watching couples resolve disputes. I also was totally unfamiliar with strong emotional reactions like the ones I saw coming from Nan, so I folded easily and judged her as selfish and untrustworthy. My assessment of my own behavior was that I was the reasonable and intelligent one; clearly the problem was her. I acted confident and like a knowledgeable expert. I used a favorite one-two-punch of controllers: I look calm and ask probing questions—some of which imply that Nan is thinking incorrectly about us. And then I used my impeccable reasoning to explain why she was wrong, and I just couldn't understand why she thought that way. Eventually, if necessary, I would get defensive and angry, and I sometimes withdrew to avoid more conflict. I'll never forget the day I realized my defensiveness was my attempt to argue my wife back into liking me!

This type of controlling, defensive, and performing coping reactivity invites Nan or others to either get angrier and escalate the conflict in order to be heard, or give up and withdraw, sometimes believing they are at fault. Ironically, such outcomes reinforce my insecurity in the relationship, fearful that I and the relationship will fail. My controlling-performer behavior got me in front of groups as a relationship expert, but on a personal level, it perpetuated feelings of insecurity, inadequacy, and fear.

NAN'S PAIN CYCLE: THE
ESCAPER-PERFORMER-SHAMER-BLAMER

Nan: I grew up in a home of toxic soup composed of depression, anxiety, fear, shame, blame, secret keeping, and anger. Family dinners consisted of my parents fighting, my sister shrinking into her seat to avoid the conflict, my other sister spilling her milk for attention to break the tension between our parents, and me on emotional overload, bursting into tears. My parents never consoled me, ever, and my dad would scream for me to "put away the water works!" Conflict was never resolved. We simply waited for the next dramatic episode.

With so much anger in my home, I learned early how to lay low, not draw attention to myself, and try not to make anyone mad. I was trying to escape the relentless attacks and open rejection from my family. But I also learned to perform to try and win my parents' approval through doing the right things and being a good girl. When escaping and performing did not work, I did what many who are emotionally abused do—I attacked myself with questions like *What's wrong with me? Why am I not good enough? Why am I so unlovable? Why do I feel so empty?* (All of them are about identity and a lack of safety.) Now I know that my parents parented out of their own pain story. They walled themselves off emotionally from me, making it easy for them to say things like I would not amount to anything. My dad was depressed and suicidal most of my life. He basically lived in the garage or basement, and was physically and emotionally unavailable to me and my sisters. It was his way of escaping my mother's anger, but as a child I experienced it as rejection and abandonment.

Nothing felt safe in our home, and everyone was on edge. We survived by the adage "every person for themselves." My sisters and I couldn't control our environment or whether or not we were loved and valued, so to escape home, we turned to friends, boyfriends, and food. We controlled what we ate. My oldest sister would eventually die at age forty-five of physical complications from anorexia.

As a young girl I loved to read fictional stories and watch TV shows in which families resolved their conflict with a group hug in less than thirty minutes. But as I got older my performing and escaping efforts shifted into bitterness, resentment, and unforgiveness toward my parents and the injustice I felt. I was aggressive in blaming, being rude, angry, and disrespectful. And that was when I met Ron. Compared to my family, his was calm, kind, and loving. Life with them was more like what I had always dreamed. So, I escaped into Ron's world and two years later we were married.

But my pain came right along with me. In Ron's family, a long heritage of ministry meant there were high expectations. All the children were high achievers. Early on, I strove to lay low and learn how to be just like them so I could fit in and not make anyone angry. Sound familiar? Evil whispered, *You're not good enough for this family and you are not minister's wife material. You better start doing more and performing well, or else...* I did everything I could to win favor and praise and prove my worth. But when escaping, laying low, performing, and trying to win approval didn't seem to work, I returned to the old familiar coping territory of blame, anger, and resentment. This was particularly evident during a season when Ron's need for achievement took over and he was physically and emotionally unavailable to me; the pattern of my pain and coping repeated itself. The more he worked, the angrier I got. The more he wanted to achieve and was absent, the more abandonment and rejection I felt. Once again, I was left feeling, *What am I doing wrong? What can I do to make you love me?*

Then came our journey into the valley of the shadow of death. Our middle son, Connor, died from an MRSA staph infection after being ill for just ten days. He was only twelve years old. Our family was devastated. I was heartbroken. It was as if everything I held dear was gone. Grief touched every aspect of my life, and even when I tried to lay low, the depression and anxiety of my past kicked into overdrive and the dark night of the soul was too much to bear. I wanted to die. I asked, "Where is God? Why is this happening?" I cried out to God, "God, I can't do this. Over thirty thousand people have been following our website posts about Connor's story and praying for him and, God, you said *no*. Why?" My identity and sense of safety were in shreds. It was hard to pray, hard to read my Bible, and hard to make it through church. When I heard songs like "It Is Well with My Soul," I just wanted to scream, *"No, it is not!"* I began repeating my patterns of coping and found ways of

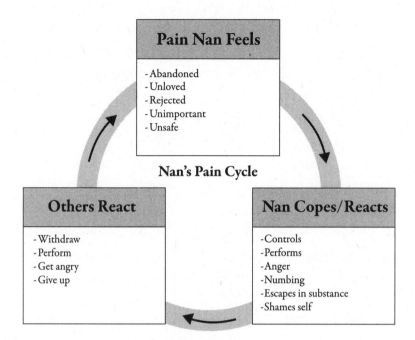

Illustration 2: Nan's Pain Cycle

escaping. What started with sleeping aids, depression medi-cation, anxiety pills, and a glass of wine to take the edge off escalated into a twelve-year addiction to over-the-coun-ter and prescription medications and more and more alco-hol. With each passing year the drinking continued and got worse, and I took larger amounts of pills to remain numb. I did not want to feel. I was so angry at God. I felt a deep sense of abandonment. I coped by getting angry, bitter, and resentful. I turned away from God and anything of Light and Truth like the Bible, prayer, or Christian music.

All of this nearly cost me our marriage.

Though the painful circumstances of my life had changed over the years, my pain cycle remained the same.

My transitions in and out of escape, performing, shaming, and blaming can be very quick or very slow. Sometimes I cycle through the whole process in minutes, and sometimes the cycle runs the course over a week or more. Either way, when I am emotionally dysregulated, how long I stay dysregulated is overwhelmingly up to me.

All four reactive coping styles are part of my process. That does not make my cycle any worse or any better than someone with one, two, or three coping reactions. They're all damaging because they are neither loving nor trustworthy. A pain cycle with one style of reactive coping can be every bit as damaging as one with all four.

FACING OURSELVES

It has taken Nan and me a long time to unpack the above narratives. It took me many years to get honest about the residue of pain on my heart, so even though I had a lot of relationship knowledge, I didn't know what to do with my own story. Even if you have clarity about pain in your life, what is vital is that you connect your pain to your coping style. Discover the neurological rut your brain gets stuck in. Recognize your old-self pattern.

What I've discovered about myself is, when I feel inadequate, I work harder to impress (control). When I feel that I've lost Nan's favor, I argue (defensiveness) or turn the tables and reject responsibility (blame).

When Nan feels unimportant, she performs (control) until she decides she can't win you over, and at that point she gets angry (control). When Nan feels abandoned, she runs to a combination of performance, anger, and numbing (escape).

CREATE YOUR PAIN CYCLE

You can put on self-control by mindfully recognizing your destructive reactions when you feel unloved or unsafe. Focus on being honest about *you*. Your pain cycle contributes to the angst in your marriage (as well as with family, friends, coworkers, and beyond). Identifying your pain cycle is a necessary first step on the path of change. (Your spouse will focus on theirs. Later, we show you how they intersect and how each of you can put on self-regulation with the four steps in the Path to Peace found in part 2: The New Self.) These research-proven principles have changed thousands of lives and marriages around the globe. Using exercise 2 on the following page (a spouse can use the copy in appendix 3), you can create your pain cycle in the graphic that follows it.

If you completed exercise 2, you have just identified and named your pain cycle. Chances are this preexisted your marriage and will exist (though in diminishing intensity as you work on it) throughout your lifetime. It's a picture of the cumulative story of pain in your life. Through determination and the power of the Spirit, you can grow beyond it. Hold it with respect. It is powerful—likely more than you realize.

For some, the words you placed in the "PAIN I FEEL" section represent a truckload of heartache and difficulty.

Exercise 2

Mapping Your Individual Pain Cycle

1. Look back at the feelings that you identified in Exercise 1 (page 33). Write those words in the first box of the Pain Cycle (page 61) under the title PAIN I FEEL.

2. Connect those emotions with the actions or coping responses from the list below. When you feel those emotions, how do you normally react?
Circle up to five *of the most common or consistent* reactions/coping that best describe what you do.

Blames Others	Shames Self	Controls	Escapes / Creates Chaos
Rage	Depressed	Perfectionists	Impulsive
Angry	Negative	Performs	Numbs Out
Sarcastic	Whines	Judgmental	Avoids Issues
Arrogant	Inconsolable	Demanding	Escapes Using Substance
Aggressive	Catastrophizing	Critical	Escapes Using Activity
Retaliatory	Manipulative	Defensive	Irresponsible
Threatening	Fearful	Anxious	Selfish
Punishing	Pouting	Intellectualizes	Minimizes
Fault Finding	Harms Self	Nagging	Addicted
Discouraging	Needy	Lecturing	Secretive
Other: _____			

3. Write the words you've circled in the Pain Cycle under the title COPES/REACTS (page 61).

4. Think about how people around you respond to you when you react in the ways described in the prior two sections. What do they usually say or do? Write up to five of those responses under the title OTHERS REACT in the Pain Cycle.

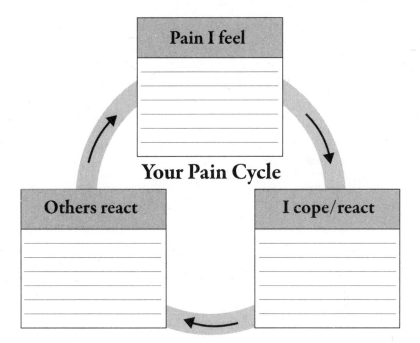

Each pain you listed has many stories behind it. In fact, you may be feeling overwhelmed at this point thinking about all they represent. Keep reading to learn how to manage your reactivity, but to unpack your stories and the residue they have left on your soul, consider sitting down with a trusted therapist or pastor.

Your pain cycle shows how you cope when dysregulated. When feeling loved and safe, it's easy to be your best self, but when love and safety are in question, your pain cycle will quickly take over.

At this point you may be wondering, *What's the solution to my pain cycle?* This was exercise 2 of 5. Keep going. In subsequent chapters we'll explore how to self-regulate when the pain cycle takes over. For now, let's make a few quick observations and reminders while you engage in the conversation questions for this chapter.

NEW SELF, PEACEFUL US CONVERSATION:

- Take some time to reflect on your pain cycle and think back through some recent occasions when you got dysregulated. Can you see a few of the emotions and reactions coming to life? Notice the sequencing of your pain, your coping, and other's reactions. Keep in mind, this pain cycle (or at least the seeds of it) likely preceded your marriage. What is the implication for your marital conflict?

- React to this: knowing your pain cycle alone doesn't bring an end to it. Becoming intimately familiar with it is the first step. Throughout your lifetime, you will continue to unpack your story of pain, what it leads you to do, and how to self-regulate.

- Getting intimately familiar with your pain cycle is an important step to growing beyond it. To that end, begin saying your pain cycle out loud. You've mapped it, but to get this awareness into other parts of your brain you need to say it out loud. Fill in the blanks to this sentence and say it aloud to yourself:

  "When I feel [name one pain], I tend to react by [name one coping]. When others see that, they often [name their reactions], which just makes me feel [name the same pain or perhaps another that arises at that point]." Keep going until you've said all of them aloud.

When you're ready, share your pain cycle with a safe, trusted friend.

It might also be helpful to write a brief narrative of your pain cycle like we did in this chapter. It doesn't have to be long; just spell out in a few sentences your pain, how you cope, and how others tend to react.

- Vulnerability is high when sharing a pain cycle. If your spouse trusts you with their pain cycle, guard your response. Like someone handing you an infant, hold it delicately and with respect for the value it has. Be trustworthy and compassionate.

- Take a picture of your pain cycle to refer to it when triggered. Having a picture on your smartphone gives you quick reference to the words (emotions and actions) that can be hard to remember when you're dysregulated.

CHAPTER 6

Your Couple Pain Cycle

The close proximity of married life gives our spouse access to us that nobody else has. We get to see things in our spouse nobody else sees. The way he brushes his teeth in tiny circles or the way she brushes her hair in a certain way. We also share a partner's greatest joys and see their worst fears. This intimate knowledge and predictability can be beautiful. It can also be confusing, especially when it's hard or unpleasant.

Marital partners are inherently vulnerable to each other. Our proximity exposes the best and worst of us to the other. How do you make sense of their "worst"? How do you interpret their blame/shame/control/escape behavior? What often gets lost in those moments is their desire for you. Indeed, for both partners, poor coping is often a failed attempt to restore love and safety to your usness. Conflict, ironically, stems from a deep desire to connect. Even worse, when one partner's failed attempt to connect intersects with the other partner's failed attempt to connect, the pain in their usness increases significantly.

"WHO STARTED IT?"

Couples rarely agree on who started their last conflict, yet once it starts, there's almost always a pattern. Partners might even be able to predict what is going to be said or done next: "This is the part when she loses her temper" or "Here is where we start criticizing one another." Or the pattern might sound something like "This is where she starts shaming herself with self-condemnation" or "Here is where one of us heads for the door and leaves." A familiar soundtrack gets played nearly every time. It can feel draining, senseless, and hopeless.

Couple conflicts are predictable because your individual pain cycles are, too. When your individual pain cycles collide, they create a *couple* pain cycle. It has a life and momentum of its own, fueled by your individual pain cycles. Stop your pain cycle (or if your spouse stops theirs) and you'll notice your couple pain cycle stops, too.

When emotionally dysregulated, you may think your conflict is because your spouse is not listening to you, refuses to change, or because he or she does not care enough about you to meet your needs. When you're dysregulated, you may think that *your spouse* is wrong, and *if they would only get themselves together, then everything would be fine.* But when we think they are dysregulated, it is almost always that we, too, are emotionally dysregulated and acting out our pain cycle.

The path to change is not to focus on their part, but yours.

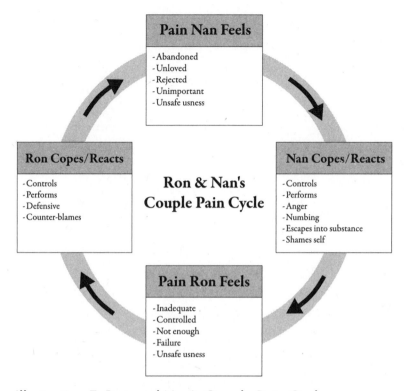

Illustration 3: Ron and Nan's Couple Pain Cycle

When addressing how we judge and condemn others, Jesus said it this way, "First take the log out of your own eye" (Matt. 7:5 ESV). Unfortunately, most of us are obsessed with the "speck" in the other's eye, especially when feeling unloved or unsafe.

Cycles don't have a beginning point (at least not one we can objectively identify). So, it's pointless to argue over who started any particular conflict. Our couple pain cycle can start anywhere.

Say Nan gets upset with me one evening for being emotionally unavailable because I'm thinking about a work project. She will likely feel *unloved and rejected* (and potentially *abandoned* if it continues over time); this speaks to her sense of worth (identity). She may also feel alone and, therefore, *unloved*. Remember, what she desires is to feel close and connected to me, and to feel my presence and investment in our relationship. Under threat, Nan's midbrain will take action to try and make that desire a reality. For her, this looks like *control and perform*. If that doesn't work, potentially she may spill over into *blame/anger, numbing/escape,* and/or *shaming herself.*

Once Nan begins acting this way, do you think I feel her desire, or her longing to be connected with me in a healthy way? Not likely. When I feel her control or anger, I feel *insecure and inadequate* and *unsafe*. I, too, want a safe usness, so I use my coping behavior to try and make things better from my point of view. But do you think *controlling* the situation or Nan's feelings, *performing* to make it up to her, or becoming *defensive and withdrawing* is going to help? Not likely. This in turn will ensure that Nan feels *unloved and rejected* as well as *abandoned and unimportant* to me. And in a millisecond, we are in an escalating cycle of conflict.

Again, it does not matter where the emotional dysregulation began—it could have started with either person. Once triggered, we start our individual pain cycle, which makes it overwhelmingly likely that our spouse will get triggered and activate their pain cycle, too, creating a couple pain cycle.

As we said earlier, our tendency is to focus on the other person in the couple pain cycle. My coping is aimed at changing Nan's coping, and her coping aims to change mine. I defend so she will stop being angry. She gets angry so I will stop performing at work and instead give her my presence and care. I then counterblame so she will stop controlling how I apply myself to work. I focus on her speck, and she focuses on mine.

This is what we do. This is what we all do—and we do it over and over and over and expect that eventually our reactive coping will make their speck disappear.

Anyone feeling the insanity yet?

To get a different result, I have to stop trying to change how Nan handles her pain. Instead, humility invites me to focus on my half of the couple pain cycle and on managing my pain in a different manner. In other words, I can stop reacting so I can mindfully respond.

We'll teach you how to mindfully respond in the next chapter. For now, let's recognize how your individual pain cycle and the couple pain cycle interact. People get emotionally dysregulated when they feel unloved, unsafe, or both. It's that simple. And because marriage is an intense and close relationship, we are prone to get into this pain cycle often. But there's a way out of pain. Once you realize that your individual pain cycle is the key to unlocking your couple pain cycle, you'll also realize that there aren't twenty or thirty conflicts to fix in your marriage. You have one issue—your pain cycle—that plays out in every conflict, in every bad moment.

WHY CAN'T WE JUST STOP?

Why do we repeat the couple pain cycle? Now that we know what happens, can't we just stop this destructive pattern? Can't we just resist the temptation and never do it again?

That's a valid question. Remember how your neurological system is wired. The mind prioritizes protecting your identity and safety. The pain story your brain has been writing through the years is wrapped around the most tender and impactful times of your life. Your brain holds on to these feelings as a vulnerability and wants to protect you from more pain.

Second, your brain is efficient. During emotional dysregulation the midbrain is wired for *fight or flight*. So, from infancy you've had limited options when emotionally dysregulated. Once those expressions are formed, we repeat them. Your reactivity—whether blame, shame, control, or escape—has been well practiced. Any challenge to your identity, safety, or both sends your brain into a routine pattern. This is why we repeat the same cycle so easily and why patterns are so tenacious. Ninety percent of the time when you are emotionally dysregulated, you fall into the pattern of your pain cycle. When that dysregulation is with your spouse, the likelihood that you'll follow the couple pain cycle is even higher.

"SECRETS" TO A HAPPY MARRIAGE

Helping marriages thrive has been my life's work. Even so, I sometimes cringe when I see how wrong the messaging around marriage is—even in Christian marriages. Erroneous messages abound. Couples arrive for counseling with complaints like, "They don't hear me or communicate."

"Every time we try and talk about anything serious or substantial, we fight." "I can never please him/her." "My needs are unheard, unmet, and ignored." "We're too different. We're incompatible."

The implicit idea underlying these complaints is that we'd be happy *if only*... if only we were more compatible, communicated better, or if only my spouse could meet my needs, I'd stop complaining about his work. There's an assumption that a partner can make me feel emotionally secure, confident, and physically satisfied. "Meet my needs" underlies nearly every complaint couples bring about communication, conflict, and not trusting their partner. And sometimes when needs go unmet, a partner feels justified abandoning the relationship to meet those needs elsewhere.

"Meet my needs" is the opposite of "take off the old self and put on the new." It's misleading and dangerous because in effect it says "You're responsible for regulating my dysregulation." Marriage isn't about cajoling, manipulating, or controlling my spouse into making me happy—and them trying to do the same to me. That's what the four coping responses fail to accomplish. Trying to make your spouse make you feel at peace in your identity and safety will never work. (To learn more about mistaken cultural perspectives on marriage and how marriage ministries inadvertently perpetuate them, visit rondeal.org/themindfulmarriage.)

Marriage is a relationship that fosters the humility of Christ; helps you learn to steward your gifts, talents, limitations, and deficits (pain cycle); and lets you develop your ability to give and receive. It is a gift that uniquely cultivates us to grow emotionally, spiritually, cognitively and physically, and become a sacrificial giver. Decades of research and therapy with couples just like you has taught us that the only way to feel like you are growing and fulfilled as a person and in a loving, safe relationship is to reckon with the hard and unlovely things about yourself (what your pain cycle reveals) while being loving and giving to your marriage. You can't *take* peace and fulfillment. You *build* peace and fulfillment. Don't worry about the growth of your spouse or whether your needs will be met; focus first on your own work. (We do recognize that sometimes partners are actively doing things that sabotage trust and your desire to give; in a later chapter we'll talk about how you respond in those situations.)

WHAT IS YOUR COUPLE PAIN CYCLE?

Matters of communication, serving the needs of your spouse, and compatibility are all more easily managed when we are emotionally regulated. Spouses easily give out of the abundance of God's love and provision when their identity is firm and sense of safety strong. Self-regulated partners manage communication hiccups well.

We've established the centrality of taking ownership of your pain. While we want you to work on your side of your couple pain cycle, it is helpful to be familiar with the complete cycle.

Mapping Your Couple Pain Cycle

Refer to your completed individual pain cycle (page 61). Talk to your spouse and decide which of you will be SPOUSE #1 and which will be SPOUSE #2. Then, on the following graphic, record the words you both identified as PAIN I FEEL and how you COPE/REACT in the appropriate box.

Your spouse's responses will be recorded on that same page. If not, ask them to share what he or she identified in those same sections of their individual pain cycle and write those in the corresponding sections of the couple pain cycle.

(If each of you has a copy of this book and is recording your thoughts separately, decide which of you will be SPOUSE #1 and SPOUSE #2 so you can be consistent in your documentation of your pain cycle.)

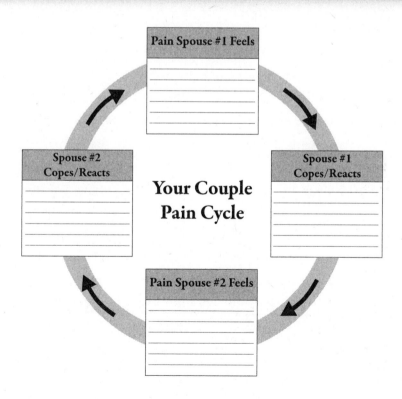

You have just identified and named your couple pain cycle.

Now, here are a few items for discussion. Let go of the idea of fixing your partner and, for now, your collective couple pain cycle. Instead, get curious about it. Your goal is to see and understand how it all fits together. If talking about it activates dysregulation, pause until you can sit with a supportive guide or counselor. A subsequent chapter will explain how to self-regulate when your pain cycle is activated and provide guidance on caring for your spouse's pain.

NEW SELF, PEACEFUL US CONVERSATION:

- On a scale of 1 to 10, how vulnerable did you feel in sharing your pain cycle with your partner? Can you identify the pain behind this vulnerability (as it relates to love and/or safety)? (This is your first chance to recognize your pain sensitivities in real time!)
- Each partner should share a story or two from early in their life when these pains and coping behaviors began to take shape (as best you can tell at this point). What happened? Looking back, what did you learn about your worth/value or lovability (identity) or your physical or emotional safety in those relationships or moments? (Partners should take great care to hear and hold the other's story with compassion. Don't try to fix it or reshape what it means to your spouse.)

- What insight have you gained about your pattern of pain and coping? Talk about your pattern and talk about a recent time it happened.
- If you currently feel safe in your usness, then with great compassion, ask questions about your partner's painful narratives.
- As you look at your couple pain cycle, acknowledge one thing you do (coping) that you now realize taps your spouse's pain. (This can be a sobering realization, but it is important to recognize and admit out loud.)

PART TWO

The New Self

CHAPTER 7

Choose to Emotionally Regulate

Chun grew up in a culture where mothers determined the parental correction and control, so in her marriage she manages the parenting for their two young children. In therapy, however, she revealed she feels alone and isolated in parenting. Her husband responded that when she corrects his parenting, he feels inadequate and shames himself.

In working on her pain cycle, she learned that excessive control flows from her own sense of failure and feeling unloved by her mother. Criticism and control are how she coped with pain throughout her childhood, and now they are creating problems in her marriage. Rather than reacting in dysregulation, she has been learning to self-regulate and respond out of her peace cycle (something you'll begin to explore in this chapter). When self-regulated, Chun responds quite differently to her children and husband, including being nurturing and calm when issues arise. Here's a fabulous example.

Chun and her family recently went on a Disney cruise. Her husband surprised her with a massage on the cruise. He made plans to take care of the kids while she enjoyed the gift. As she was preparing to leave the massage room, she checked her mobile phone and saw a message from Disney Cruise Line that read, "Jane has been found." Jane was their four-year-old daughter. Immediately Chun panicked. She felt angry, scared, and critical of her husband. However, using the four steps you are about to learn, she was able to process her pain. She activated humility and her peace cycle. When she met back up with her husband, she greeted him with a touch on his arm and said, "That must have been difficult." (A pleasant surprise for him!) In her old self, she would have approached him with anger and accusation. In her new self, she was able to move toward him and connect with his pain, and then listen to the story of what had happened—which was, in fact, alarming and difficult for him.

Later, when Chun reported this moment of victory to her therapist, she noted that her new self responded to her husband from a place of peace and compassion. It completely flipped a switch in their marriage. The rest of the cruise was extremely enjoyable and a very positive family experience.

Can you imagine this mother's pain when reading, "Jane has been found"? But staying in that pain was up to her. With humility and self-regulation, she chose a peaceful path. And that's transforming their marriage.

Let us summarize what you've learned so far so we can turn the corner and talk about what you can do about it. Restoration Therapy is based on learning that our old self is in part composed of a pain story that our brain has been writing our entire life. Instead of being rooted in the story of God pursuing us through Christ with an everlasting love— something that declares our absolute worth and safety—our pain narrative is based on imperfect earthly relationships. Many of those relationships have been loving and fulfilling in ways, but they still lacked perfection. Disappointment, fear, questions about our worth and feeling unloved, and being betrayed by those most important to us end up creating pains we remain hypersensitive to throughout our lives. At some point (for some even in infancy) we began trying to make the pain go away. Our coping strategies solidified within our mind and body in the form of neuropathways that our brain came to prefer whenever we became triggered. This pain cycle activates anytime we feel a measure of threat to our identity or sense of safety, but especially within an intimate relationship such as marriage. When couples are at their best, they love and serve each other from the best of themselves. But when at their worst, couples inadvertently trigger one another's pain cycles resulting in escalating cycles of hurt, threat, and reactivity. Because marriage is the most intimate of relationships, it inadvertently combines the individual pain cycles of each partner to create a couple pain cycle.

In this chapter, we're laying the groundwork for the four-step process you'll learn in chapter 9, which moves each partner out of their pain and your usness into peace. The good news is that we can be transformed by the renewing of our minds. We can learn to take off that old self and put on a new self that is being renewed by God's truth.

Chun coped with childhood feelings of imperfection and

being unloved with control and criticism. She controlled her husband through high expectations and criticism. When it seemed he'd missed the mark as a father, she had a choice. She could remain stuck in her pattern of control (old self) or she could choose self-control.

THE VIRTUE OF SELF-CONTROL

Are you familiar with the Marvel superhero Hulk? Behind the green giant is the brilliant scientist Bruce Banner, who, when angered or provoked, transforms into the rage-fueled, green-skinned monster known as Hulk. Dr. Banner doesn't like who he becomes, so he works hard to not get angry (what triggers his decline into Hulk).

There comes a time in the 2012 Marvel movie, *The Avengers*, when the team needs Bruce Banner to transform into Hulk.

"Now might be a really good time for you to get angry," says Captain America.

"That's my secret, Cap," replies Banner. "I'm always angry."

I'll never forget that line because until that moment I thought Banner was a victim of his anger, that he had no control over it. But when I saw this conversation with Captain America, I realized he could manage his pain and anger because he knew how to self-regulate.

You and I have a Hulk inside us that is released by pain. And it likes to smash (Hulk's favorite word). But we can learn how to self-regulate. The Bible calls this self-control.

Self-control is mindful restraint (or control) over one's

own impulses, emotions, thoughts, and behaviors. There are times when impulses and emotions rule. Thus, self-control is the virtue of being able to keep yourself—your best-balanced self—in control of making decisions. Self-control is a fruit of the Spirit (Gal. 5:22–23 ESV). When you are in high conflict with your spouse, self-control is difficult. In emotional dysregulation, impulses press you to say or do destructive things. N. T. Wright, the noted theologian, says that self-control is the only virtue that we cannot fake. Even if someone is good at faking virtue, when dysregulated they will not be calm, peaceful, or in charge of themselves. Self-control is stabilizing emotionally without relying on environment or others to help.

Like all the virtues found in the fruits of the Spirit, self-control helps us be our best selves. Self-control is not white-knuckling it to avoid harmful words or actions; it is replacing dysregulation with peace and calm. It is a peace where you feel at ease with who you are and feel empowered to handle the moment that is in front of you. And that kind of peace mobilizes you to move to other virtues like kindness, gentleness, faithfulness, and love, as 2 Peter 1:5–7 describes: "For this very reason, make every effort to supplement your faith with virtue, and virtue with knowledge, and knowledge with self-control, and self-control with steadfastness, and steadfastness with godliness, and godliness with brotherly affection, and brotherly affection with love" (ESV). When peaceful and self-regulated, your gifts, talents, and strengths are unleased to love well and experience wholehearted intimacy.

Now here's the problem. We've all heard good sermons about self-control, the fruit of the Spirit, and loving our enemies. But how do we actually do it, especially when dys-regulated by our pain?

SELF-REGULATING YOUR EMOTIONS: GET CENTERED IN THE TRUTH

Your best self—the part of you that is peaceful, gifted, and loving—is already in you. Why do you think your spouse fell in love with you in the first place? Sure, it gets covered up with your pain cycle when you are emotionally out of whack, but it does not mean it is not there. When we put on self-control and emotionally self-regulate, we reconnect with who we are and who we're made to be. *You have the ability and responsibility of stabilizing and regulating your own identity and safety.* In self-control you stabilize your identity in how precious you are to God, for example, to find peace even in stressful situations. If you remind yourself how much your spouse, friends, or family love you, you can put on self-control even during chaos. If you stabilize to know that no matter how unsafe the world is, you are empowered to move things and relationships in a positive direction, you will be able to mobilize yourself with actions that are constructive, loving, and giving.

ROOTED IN TRUTH

God's truth is that we are loved, forgiven, cherished, and prized by the Father. So why do we react out of pain instead of responding out of this truth? Our brains are prone to notice the negative instead of the positive,[1] and it's twice as likely to hold on to negative messages than positive ones. Negative messages stick in the brain like Velcro while positive messages are like Teflon—they are nonstick.[2]

Both Nan and I can relate to that. My pain causes me to wonder whether I really measure up as a professional, for example. That feeling persists despite many accomplishments, writing and contributing to more than twenty books and resources for couples and families, and gaining the respect of many of my peers. Fear is not rational. I can't argue it into deciding if I've done enough or are enough. Abandonment is a pain Nan has experienced many times in her life. But even though we've been married since 1986 and I've repented of being a workaholic (a season when I did emotionally abandon her), she still fears from time to time that work is my number one love and that it will get all of me.

These beliefs are not rooted in truth. They have grown in our brains out of pain.

To combat this, get centered in God's truth. God has given you self-control. God will not exercise control over you. Believe what he says about you (see chapter 2). Embrace the truth of who you are in God and claim it for your own. Then, set about attacking your sinful old nature that drives your pain cycle. Authoritatively and confidently claim truth for yourself. You are the most powerful speaker of the truth about your identity and sense of safety when it comes to deciding your behavior, emotional regulation, and actions. Get centered in the truth.

Maybe sometimes you believe what God says about you and sometimes you don't. When life is okay, calm and safe in God's hands, it is easier to be at peace. But when you're dysregulated, pain cycles kick in. Go "vertical" in such moments to remember divine truth. That's how self-regulation begins.

REJECTING THE LIE

In your pain cycle (exercise 2, page 60) you identified "Pain I Feel." *These feelings are lies we have told ourselves and keep alive about our identities and safety.* We must be aggressive with these lies. In my case, I must put to death the insecurity and fear I feel around not being enough. Nan must refuse to entertain the idea that she is unloved, rejected, and abandoned.

Mindfulness helps us actively reject lies. It essentially involves taking captive old-self lies and replacing them with truth—and the actions that accompany them. In Philippians 4:8 Paul puts it this way: Think about what is good (true, pure, and lovely) then put it into action, and the God of peace will be with you.

Taking lies captive starts by calling them *out loud*. Make a firm and dramatic statement. For example, "I refuse to believe I am unloved, unwanted, and not enough." Speaking aloud is a more dramatic experience than internal thinking. Use *repetition*. Negative thoughts and beliefs are sticky like Velcro in the brain. Rebuking them aloud several times a day tells your brain you mean business. Start there. Later in the book, we'll teach you the four steps that make up the Path to Peace. They build off these ideas and create an even more powerful change experience with lasting results.

EMBRACING THE TRUTH

It is not enough to just confront the lie. Embrace the truth. Again, it's a matter of attention (mindfulness). Set your mind on the things of the Spirit (Rom. 8:5–6). For instance, "I am chosen, loved, and cherished." The truth will calm you. It will center you in peace. Embracing the truth does not dismiss your pain. Rather it focuses your mind on reassuring, comforting, and confidence-building truths. Over time, and with practice, your identity and sense of safety will be bolstered, and your emotional stability will grow.

Begin embracing the truth about you and developing your peace cycle by doing exercise 4 (next page).

Once you have completed exercise 4, you have begun rewriting a narrative of love and safety over your life, take another step of mindfulness. *Experience* the truth. Imagine yourself sitting in a chair a few feet in front of you. Take a minute to visualize yourself in that chair. Now, address yourself as a loving and caring parent. Hear yourself say words like, "You are precious to me and deeply loved. You are enough for any task life sets before you. You are never alone." Incorporate words from exercise 4 and make specific statements to yourself in the chair. Feel them hit your heart and speak to your pain. If you have trouble imagining yourself as a loving parent, stand in front of a mirror. Speak

---
Exercise 4

Identifying Self-Regulating Truths

Think about the words that can emotionally regulate the painful lies about yourself, your identity, and your sense of safety. Which words below are meaningful and powerful to you because they represent the truth about your identity and safety? Choose words that directly repudiate the lies your pain cycle has been telling you. For example, if one of your painful feelings was "Unloved," then you might circle "Worthy" (of being loved) below. If you feel "Inadequate," you might circle "Enough."

(Circle three to five words that you would like to be able to claim as your own that would be representative of the new reality or truth about your identity and sense of safety.)

Loved	Worthy	Significant	Not Alone	Prized
Valuable	Precious	Adequate	Approved	Accepted
Wanted	Appreciated	Hopeful	Free	Safe
Secure	Sure	Fulfilled	Capable	Empowered
In Control	Protected	Connected	Intimate	Competent
Validated	Successful	Enough		

Other: _____

These words are your Emotionally Regulating Truths.

to yourself as the person you are on your strongest, wisest, most secure day. Say your truths confidently and calmly out loud just as if you were encouraging a friend, coworker, or teammate. Experience is powerful when it comes to changing the brain. The out-loud experience helps you embrace the truth more, as does *repetition*. The more you hear yourself say these regulating truths, the more likely you will be able to reject the lies and tell yourself the truth about your identity and sense of safety. (Daily saying the structured Humility Shift statement found in appendix 1 helps to plant seeds of truth in your brain and heart.)

At times we hear these truth words from our spouse, parents, or a trusted person in our life, and it is helpful to hear the truth. This affirmation is good when it comes without manipulation; however, your own affirmation of the truth to yourself is more powerful. The mind typically discounts secondary opinions—even if they are from the person you long to affirm you the most. Your voice is the strongest voice in your head. God has great things to say about your identity and sense of safety, but you must choose to hear and acknowledge His truth for you. And when you embrace God's truths over you, you begin to put pain to death and live out of peace.

Darius moved to the United States with his family as an infant. In their move to the States, his family worked hard to maintain the Egyptian characteristics of family they cherished, such as loyalty to the family of origin and communal living. When Rebecca met Darius, she loved his traditional sense of family and commitment to his parents and siblings. The couple talked about this cultural difference. Although they loved his family, they decided they would not live with them once they married. They wanted a strong relationship with his family and valued the traditions of Darius's family but wanted to have their own lifestyle. Walking this out was more difficult than it seemed.

Once they married, Rebecca began to feel that she wasn't as important to Darius as his family. After having their first baby, Darius left to check on his aging parents, which made Rebecca feel alone and unimportant. She knew Darius loved her and was very committed to her and their family. Reminding herself of that truth was vital. As she drove to work each morning, she repeated to herself out loud that Darius leaving to take care of his parents was, for him, an act of love toward not just them, but the whole family. "And," she said to herself, "that is something I value as well." She did ask Darius to go when it fit into her schedule, and on occasion she went with him. Because they both valued commitment to caring for their parents, moving toward him in those moments strengthened their relationship. His willingness to modify his parental visits to times that were mindful of Rebecca affirmed that she was his priority. Rebecca chose to focus on the truth of being loved and important and on choosing actions in line with that truth. This opened the door for their family to grow together in ways that built strong generational ties.

COREGULATION OR SELF-REGULATION?

Being dependent on your partner to regulate your emotions or meet your needs is called *emotional coregulation*. And to some degree, it is helpful. Having someone we love, value, and trust give us care and attention generally does make us feel safe and better about ourselves. It certainly is how children are emotionally regulated. After all, when we are young and just forming our identities and sense of safety, it is most often our primary caregivers that pull close to us, listen to us, say comforting things, and assure us they are there for us and love us. A hungry or cold infant who is suckled by their mother, for example, can calm down through the coregulation of the parent. This is a good metaphor of what children need emotionally throughout their childhood from the important people in their life. This is totally natural and appropriate—*for children*.

But as we grow, maturity demands that we learn to self-sooth and emotionally stabilize ourselves. When entering the presence of the Lord in worship, the writer of Psalm 131:2 says, "I have calmed and quieted my soul, like a weaned child with its mother; like a weaned child is my soul within me" (ESV). The author has learned to regulate himself so his heart is in the right place before the Lord. He is no longer a dependent child; he is an adult. You see, emotional coregulation, while totally appropriate for children, is not a great strategy for married adults. To expect our spouse to take the place of some former parental figure who failed us is to say, "I am inadequate to care for myself and I need you to be emotionally stable and healthy so I will be okay."

Now, listen closely: There are many who teach this, though they don't realize it, and others who would say, "That is exactly right and that is what marriage is about." But we do not agree. This kind of emotional dependency and connection is much more like *parenting* than it is *partnering*. And who wants to make love to an emotional child, or parent?

A parent gives and gives and does not expect anything in return from a child; it is a lopsided relationship because it is the job of the parent to meet the child's needs until the child gradually reaches maturity. Partnering, on the other hand, is where two adults bind themselves together in mutual pledges of sacrifice, work, and enjoying life together side by side. Intimacy in marriage is formed by *sharing* and *mutuality*. In parenting, intimacy is limited to a one-sided affair where the parent knows almost everything about the child, but the child is just the beneficiary of the parent's care. There is no obligation for the child to give back (until the parent reaches old age). This is not a good system for marriage.

The model that we much prefer for marriage is the one you've been learning, *self-regulation*. It is where I, as a partner, take charge of my own identity and empower myself around my sense of safety, stabilize my emotions about the truth of who I am and my circumstance, then put myself in an emotionally adult (not needy or demanding) position to work with, problem-solve, and share with my spouse. If you want a relationship that is based on meeting your needs, you will always be looking for a parent, that is, a spouse who helps you emotionally regulate. If you want a partnership, then make use of the tools you are learning to help you self-regulate your pain and coping so you can companion with your spouse, not be dependent on them.

That last point is critical. Coregulation is helpful, but it is not transformative. As we experience the bumps and bruises of life, your spouse can offer you a calming, reassuring presence temporarily (and we hope they do), but they aren't powerful enough to significantly transform your sense of identity and safety or how you react to pain. That is something only self-regulation, through the power of the Holy Spirit, can do.[3]

Notice, the agency in what we just said. No, you cannot control your spouse and there's no guarantee that they will grow up in the manner we are suggesting. But when you take agency of your life, when you stop acting like a needy infant and mature as a partner, the likelihood of your usness maturing as well goes up considerably. No one can guarantee you complete love and safety in your marriage, but self-regulation makes it much more likely.

Coregulation is part of all relationships and serves us to a point. But we should not be dependent on it. What are we saying to single people when we suggest that coregulation is how married individuals find fulfillment? Where does that leave them? Self-regulation is a personal maturity that is not based on marital status; it empowers people to give the best of themselves in all their relationships.

Healthy people can be in coregulating relationships while also practicing self-regulation when they're dysregulated. Being around people who engender safe feelings soothes our nervous system, making it easy to respond in safe and loving ways. It's a peace cycle of giving and receiving emotional safety.[4] Coregulating relationships within extended family, church community, friendships, and work environment also contribute to overall mental health. But in moments of dysregulation, the most urgent need is for self-regulation. Coregulation cannot help us get past our own pain; only self-regulation (self-control) can do that.

One final thought: since coregulation is the goal of therapy for some counselors and is taught by most marriage ministries (even though they don't realize it), you may have to inform them of the advantages of self-regulation. Learn more about how to do so (and how self-regulation speaks to communication training, the Enneagram, love languages, etc.) at rondeal.org/themindfulmarriage.

AN EMPOWERED CHOICE

When we self-regulate and stabilize our emotions around identity and safety with the truth, we can choose to respond differently. This gives us what we call *an empowered choice.*

In other words, when you calm yourself with the words of truth (which you picked out in exercise 4), you can take a deep breath, drink in the truth, and take the next right step into actions corresponding with that truth. In particular, actions that are more loving and trustworthy. Instead of reacting in *blame*, you can choose to *nurture* your partner by listening to them, accepting them, and encouraging their heart because you're not relying on them to take care of you. Rather than following your pain and shaming yourself, you can choose to *value self.* Rather than protecting yourself through the manipulation of *control*, you can seek a *balance of mutual give-and-take* in the relationship. Instead of escaping what feels like a lack of safety by retreating, being absent, avoiding, or numbing yourself with behaviors or substances, you can *reliably connect*, trusting that your investment will move the relationship toward safety.

And each time you take action based on the truth, it gets easier and easier as the story of pain in your brain is rewritten with a new story. Over time, the old story diminishes and a new story—a new self—emerges.

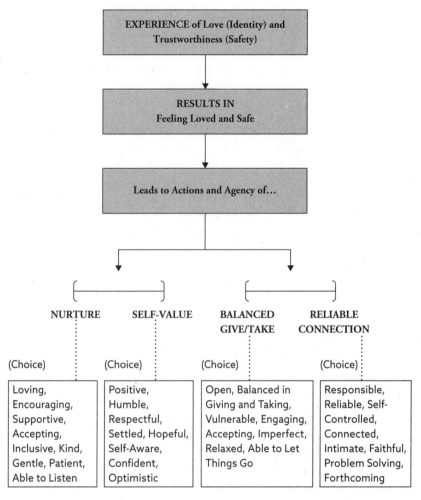

Illustration 4: Understanding Peace and Actions of Agency

Nothing good comes from a pain cycle. It perpetuates violations into further violations of ourselves and others. The absolute opposite is true of what we call the *peace cycle*. The peace cycle is not wishful thinking or simply finding a way to avoid arguments. It is a spiraling upward of loving and trustworthy actions that grow from the truth about your worth and safety. It strengthens us to be more like Christ.

You're about to identify your couple peace cycle. Here is Nan's and mine for an example.

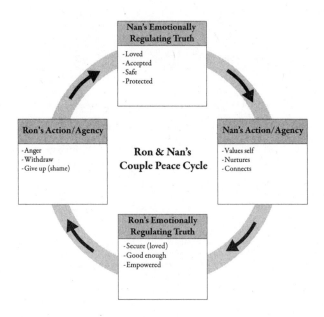

Illustration 5: Ron and Nan's Couple Peace Cycle

When we self-regulate, instead of reacting out of pain, we spiral upward into more loving and trustworthy actions. When we self-regulate, our pain cycle is almost impossible to maintain for any length of time. For instance, when Nan says out loud that she is indeed loved by God and safe in his care, and then she says out loud the general truth that I love her (even though I may not be acting in a loving way at the moment), and she lets those words experientially soak into her heart, she is then free to move emotionally toward me, even when irritated at me, and let go of trying to control me. And when I get centered in God's truth for me, I can let go of any disappointment I see in her eyes and remind myself that despite her hurt or anger in any given moment, she isn't going anywhere. I am indeed safe. This empowers me to calm down, listen and validate her pain or frustration, and trust the process. I can even admit my faults more readily because I've come to trust that they aren't going to destroy our peace.

And here's the bonus: when each of us self-regulates and responds from truth, the actions we take feed positive truth into the other. When Nan is frustrated but moves toward me, I feel safer. It's not her job to make me feel safe—again, it's my job to self-regulate. But it helps to experience connection. Likewise, when I regulate and respond out of truth with my attunement, listening ear, and openness, Nan experiences further affirmation of her worth. In these moments, self-regulation flows into coregulation, and our usness is nurtured and cared for.

The peace cycle helps us be our best self—indeed, a more mature version of the person our spouse fell in love with in the first place. It helps us follow Jesus, loving our neighbor as ourselves (James 2:8).

YOUR COUPLE PEACE CYCLE

Your pain cycle is the predictable pattern behind most of the conflicts and disconnections in your relationship. Your peace cycle helps you interrupt that pattern and move in a direction that strengthens your usness. Complete exercise 5.

Exercise 5

New Actions Based on Truth

Look back at the truths you identified in Exercise 4. Concentrate on these words, and let the reality of these truths about your identity and safety soak in. Write these words below so you can remember them easily.

_____

Talk to your spouse. On the following page, record the words you both identified as EMOTIONALLY REGULATING TRUTH from exercise 4 in the appropriate box (spouse #1 or spouse #2).

Now look at the list of words below that describe different actions/agency. When you are focused on the truth, what behaviors/actions would you likely take or choose to do? **(Circle two to five action/agency words that best describe what you would choose to do when you are in your truth and feel a sense of peace. Choose words that directly oppose the actions you take when you are in pain.)**

Loving	Values Self	Balanced Give/Take	Responsible
Encouraging	Respects Self	Vulnerable	Reliable
Supportive	Positive	Open	Self Controlled
Inclusive	Flexible	Engaging	Connected
Kind	Optimistic	Appreciative	Intimate
Listening	Hopeful	Gentle	Faithful
Accepting	Self-Aware	Relaxed	Forthcoming
Patient	Confident	Lets Things Go	Problem Solving
Compassionate	Affirming	Nurturing	

Other: _____

Record the words you circled above in your ACTION/AGENCY space on the next page. Talk to your spouse and record their words in their space.

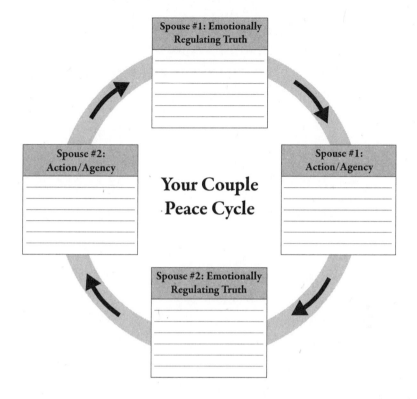

You have just identified and named your couple peace cycle.

In addition to the mindfulness tools discussed above that help you respond out of truth, in the next chapter we'll walk you through a four-step process that actively moves you out of your pain cycle and into your peace cycle. It is a proven and powerful process that has brought hope and peace to thousands of relationships.

MINDFULNESS AND PRACTICE IS THE KEY

Now, before giving you a chance to discuss your couple peace cycle, we want to warn you not to misuse the pain and peace cycles. We, at times, have misused them rather in ways that did not help us self-regulate. Instead, they became weapons that increased our dysregulation and inflicted more damage. And we've seen others do the same. Here are the top perversions of the pain and peace cycles.

Misuse #1: "Oh, This Is So Insightful. I Am Sure It Will Change Everything."

By far, this is the most common misuse of the pain and peace cycles tool. The reasoning goes something like this: "Since I (we) now understand each other's pain and peace cycles, that knowledge alone will help us avoid conflicts in the future." In other words, this is the belief that knowledge, understanding, and insight will produce the change we want. We wish that were true.

Your pain cycle is a highly charged, efficient, and automatic neurological reaction that is ingrained into your brain. A simple understanding of that sequence is in no way powerful enough to change your emotional fight-or-flight reactivity. It takes mindful concentration and alertness so that when your pain cycle is triggered, you slow yourself down intentionally and respond differently. And you must do it repeatedly to create a new self. The next chapter will provide more specific direction about how to do this.

Let us add this quick thought: The pain and peace cycles are not meant to help you avoid conflict with your spouse. This is not about squashing all conflict. It is about managing yourself during conflict. There is no way to avoid all conflict;

good marriages are not evidenced by a lack of conflict. You will be emotionally triggered at some point; it is inevitable in intimate relationships. We'll go as far to say that being triggered is a good thing because the more dysregulated you get, the more opportunities you'll have to move toward self-regulation through the peace cycle. You need the grind of this process to become a more emotionally mature person.

Misuse #2: "I Know What You Are Doing. You Are in Your Pain Cycle."

Pointing out when your spouse is in their pain cycle is a common misstep made by couples we work with, and we certainly understand the tendency. The reasoning goes like this: *I know my spouse's pain cycle so well it will be helpful for me to point it out to them so they can stop it.* Saying something like that is almost a lead-pipe cinch to drive your spouse into a full-blown pain cycle! Emotional self-regulation means just that—your spouse needs to do their own work. Yes, because your pain cycles are intimately connected (couple pain cycle), their dysregulation will likely trigger yours, and yours will trigger theirs. But stay in your lane. Do your work, not theirs.

Misuse #3: "If You Cared for Our Relationship, You Would Stop Your Pain Cycle."

This misuse is a derivative of the previous misuse in that it involves us being more concerned about, and more of an expert on, our spouse's pain cycle than our own. But instead of trying to be helpful, we use it as a weapon. This flows from a central belief that our spouse and their pain cycle are the *real problem* in the marriage. "I may have a pain cycle, but my spouse's pain cycle is ten times worse and causes all the problems." Pride is often behind this—and it only invites more angst into your usness (we will come back to this in a later chapter). For now, you must recognize that your pain cycle is just as destructive, and you must reckon with yourself and practice taking off that old self and putting on the new self.

One more derivative of this mind-set is the idea that *I would never get into my pain cycle if my spouse didn't get into theirs first.* This misuse is simply an effort to insulate ourselves from the real work we need to do on ourselves, and to weaponize our knowledge of our partner's pain cycle.

Misuse #4: "You Have Done or Said Something That Has Triggered My Pain Cycle."

This is really one of our favorites. The logic goes something like this: You have done or said something to emotionally trigger my pain cycle, so it is now your responsibility to: (1) put up with my blame, shame, control, or escape because, after all, *you caused it*; or (2) do something to get me out of my pain cycle. The purpose of the pain and peace cycles is for you to take charge of your own emotions and *self-regulate*, not justify your reactive behavior by saying your spouse is responsible for it and manipulate them to *emotionally coregulate you.* Essentially you are deciding to stay in your pain cycle until your spouse apologizes.

But here's the deal: you are an adult and as such, you are the only one who has the ability and the responsibility to move from your triggered pain to the peace cycle.

NEW SELF, PEACEFUL US CONVERSATION:

- On a scale of 1 to 10, how hopeful does your couple peace cycle make you feel about your usness? If there's a part of you that holds doubt about its ability to improve your relationship, give voice to the pain that is speaking. You are probably very familiar with that pain at this point but give voice to it anyway so you can be mindful of how it continues to cast a shadow on change.

- Let each partner talk about the truth they have identified for themselves and why it's significant to their sense of identity and safety in life and your marriage. Assuming you feel safe, speak these truths over yourself so you can experience yourself beginning to claim them. Partners should tune in to the truth their spouse is claiming. Celebrate and affirm what this might mean for them.

- Share a time when you spontaneously acted out your peace cycle. Perhaps share a time when you saw that happen in your spouse—and celebrate it!

- Review the four misuses of the pain and peace cycles. Speaking for yourself only, which have you been guilty of?
- Share any further insights you're gaining into your pain cycle and now what you seek to do about it (peace cycle).

CHAPTER 8

The Path to Peace: The Four Steps

In this chapter we're shifting from theory to practice by sharing a four-step process to systematically move you from pain to peace and a more peaceful usness.

Nan and I love to travel. We love seeing new sights, experiencing new foods, and taking in God's beauty together. Our pain cycle diminished our joy of traveling together for a long time. As ministry doors began to open for me to do seminars around the country, I worked hard to excel at every opportunity. I obsessed over prepping for seminars and traveled extensively (usually leaving Nan at home with our young children), going the extra mile for clients. On my returns home, I didn't emotionally unhook from the trip, ruminating on improvements ("How can I make it better?"). I was emotionally unavailable to Nan before, during, and after each trip. That triggered her abandonment pain, which kicked in her control and anger coping to bring me back. I resisted her control. She fought harder. I criticized her for not caring about my "Kingdom" work. This cycle went on for a decade. As my publishing and speaking career expanded, and Nan could travel with me to exotic places, we were often in conflict. It was ironic: while teaching about healthy family dynamics, our usness suffered before, during, and after the seminar. At times we traveled to weeklong marriage and family events, struggling in our usness during the entire thing.

Our inability to manage our pain even sabotaged vacation travel. Again, given my concern about disappointing others, I often engaged in work while on family vacation. When I did, Nan tried to get me to put it down so I could be emotionally present for her and our kids, but I let my anxiety keep me from completely unhooking from work tasks—essentially making me unavailable. We loved many things about the vacation travel, but we found ourselves emotionally distant and anxious about our usness throughout.

All of this has changed since we discovered how to exit dysregulation through humility and Terry Hargrave's four steps (what you'll learn in this chapter). On business trips I now recognize that my desire for the approval of others is an idol that supplants my identity in Christ, and my fear of inadequacy is not realistic given the gifts that God has granted me as a speaker and trainer. The truth is God has gone before me, so I do not have to fear. Nan has learned to trust, first and foremost, that her identity is in Christ and that she is safe in his care. He will never leave her nor forsake her. She also knows that I care and will set aside things that disconnect me from her. She also manages her control coping behavior and doesn't micromanage my thoughts, my time, or what she believes are things that will put a wedge in our usness. And when engaged in ministry travel, she is patient while I'm serving, sees and is sensitive to my anxiety and need for approval, and asks for us time when I'm done. She supports my calling and seeks balance for our usness. A new truth about our usness that we have both come to trust is that each of us will take measures to manage our pain and actively look for ways to connect with the other.

Living out of these new truths has utterly transformed our travel together. We are relaxed, connected, and able to engage each other and the trip. Of course, triggers still happen (triggers don't stop; it's how we manage them that is important). But even then, we can process our dysregulation so differently that it doesn't escalate and sabotage our time together or the trip.

PUTTING IT ALL TOGETHER: THE PAIN CYCLE PROBLEM

Imagine you could *respond to* one another out of truth, just as we shared above, instead of *reacting at* one another out of pain. Believe us, it makes all the difference.

We use the word "at" intentionally. Pain makes us react *at* one another, not with understanding or compassion or patience or kindness, but with a strong, emotionally driven reaction aimed at changing the other person and the interactions between us; essentially, we're trying to make our pain stop, or at least decrease. If you're like me, you like to think of yourself as an intellectual person—a person of reason and sound mind. But when pain hijacks my mind, I become infantile. In nanoseconds you and I both stop responding out of love; we are slaves to our pain, demanding our partners love us as we want to be loved. Pain brings out the worst in us.

Reflect once again on your pain cycle. Look closely at your pain. *Speak the pain aloud.* Mine (Ron) are Inadequate. Disapproval. Controlled. An unsafe us. *Now examine the desire behind each pain.* For me, behind "inadequate" is a need to be good enough in other people's eyes—more than that, to impress. If I win praise, I win my worth. That, of course, is the lie my pain has told me most of my life. Being "controlled" is painful because it feels like I've lost my independence and can't have what I want. All of which makes me believe I'm in an unsafe relationship that will consume me. *And what do you do when you feel that pain?* I try to *control* others' perceptions of me by performing, excelling, impressing; I try to win approval and to gain value. I defend myself to my wife whose approval means the most to me, argue with her (i.e., argue her into liking me), and if necessary, blame her (as if that will take the heat off myself).

Now, it's your turn. *Say aloud your pain and the reactive coping it leads you to do.* Look back at your individual pain cycle for a minute (chapter 5 or appendix 3). Once again speak your pain. Next, speak your coping behaviors. How are your pain and coping connected? What triggers your pain most often? Saying this out loud may be extremely painful in and of itself (much of our pain is hard to say out loud). Don't rush this. An honest appraisal is always the first step to change. You've said this out loud before, but each time you become intimately familiar with your pain.

Congratulations! You've just done the first two steps of the four-step change process. More on this in a moment, but for now, recognize that it takes humility to articulate your old self; doing so makes it more likely you can grow beyond it.

You don't have to react out of pain anymore. Imagine a day your pain is triggered, but it doesn't control you. You can respond in a healthy way rooted in God's truth. Wouldn't that be a good day? But there's even more benefit.

HUMILITY AND THE FOUR STEPS

God responds with grace toward the humble. In fact, in Jesus' words, God exalts them. When we bow our heart in humility, he lifts us up. But if we lift ourselves (e.g., try to elevate our status), he humbles us.[1] We believe this principle not only works "vertically" (or spiritually), it extends to human relationships as well ("horizontal" relationships). Showing pride toward our spouse invites their opposition, not their grace.[2]

But, when in humility, I stop trying to change or address the speck in my spouse's eye, and instead deal with the log in my eye, my self-control makes it more likely that my spouse will respond to me with grace and, in turn, examine their log as well. (For a full discussion of the pride/humility dynamic in all relationships, visit rondeal.org/themindfulmarriage for free bonus material.)

To help foster humility on a daily basis, Terry has created

a formal Humility Shift exercise. It's a daily reminder of the truth about you. See appendix 1.

Okay, you've already said the first two steps about your old self. Let's add steps three and four.

FOUR STEPS

RT taught Nan and me four steps to respond in a healthy way when triggered. All the exercises you've done to this point have prepared you to take all four.

Start with a deep breath. Mindfully calm yourself. Slow your breathing and heart rate. The vagus nerve (part of the parasympathetic nervous system) is connected to your lungs and heart. When you breathe deeply and slow your heart rate, you're communicating to your body via your vagus nerve safety it doesn't yet feel.[3] Triggers activate your body with energy to fight or flee; you can choose otherwise. In dysregulation, words can be hard to come by, so try to be gentle with yourself and take your time. Then speak aloud the four steps and make them yours.[4]

Some find it helpful to start by saying, "What I know about me is…" That simple sentence starter roots you. It also signals to your partner that you're striving for self-regulation. It's a hopeful change in tempo and tone.

Simply put, the four steps are:

1. *Say what you feel* (usually at least one feeling from the "Pain I Feel" identified in your pain cycle, found toward the end of chapter 5).

2. *Say what you normally do with that pain (coping)* (see your "Copes/Reacts" list, your pain cycle, found toward the end of chapter 5).

3. *Say the truth* (see your "Emotionally Regulating Truth" from your couple peace cycle, found at the end of chapter 7).

4. *Say what you will do differently based on this truth* (see your Action/Agency list from your couple peace cycle in chapter 7, page 99).

It's that simple.

Steps 1 and 2 proclaim your old-self pain cycle. Steps 3 and 4 speak to the new self-controlled, truth-driven peace cycle you are humbly moving toward.

Here's an example from my life that I've practiced aloud now hundreds of times (Ron), oftentimes after I've already spoken a few defensive or controlling remarks.

(Deep breath) *What I know about me is:*
   1. *I feel inadequate and unsafe.*
   2. *I get defensive and want to control the situation.*
   3. *The truth is, I'm loved by my Father and my worth is found in being His child. You still love me—in fact I've learned that you're reaching for me right now—and we'll be okay.*
   4. *I'm going to stop defending myself. Instead, I'm calming down and going to listen for your pain and try to see and hear you.*

Notice step 3 speaks directly against my pain. My knee-jerk

reactivity slows; I'm refocused and open to new possibilities. I exit pain and choose peace.

Step 4 tells Nan what to expect of me in the moment. Your couple pain cycle is very powerful; it pulls you into a familiar negative pattern of behavior with each other. Saying—*and then doing*—behavior that is more loving and emotionally safe helps to break that cycle.

At first, I could hardly see straight when Nan and I were dysregulated. It was hard to put my words together in an organized way. It took intentional focus—and practice—to get the hang of it. It helped when I practiced these four steps in moments when I wasn't dysregulated because it helped train my brain and form new neural pathways to replace my old neurological ruts. Over time the new habit strengthens pathways for loving and constructive behavior.

Tips for Implementing the Four Steps
- Take a picture of your pain and peace cycles and review them often so you can pull the words to mind when it comes time to use the four steps.
- Write out a couple versions of your typical four steps using different pain and coping words, and the corresponding truth and new action responses.
- Record yourself speaking your four steps. Then listen as you replay them for repetition to retrain your brain.

The more you practice the four steps, the easier it becomes. An economy of words is helpful. The more words you use, the more confused you and your partner may become. You're both likely dysregulated at the same time, after all. Slow the pace of your words, lower your voice and volume, and change your tone to ensure they see humility coming through as you say them.

LISTENING WELL

What an odd experience it was for me when Nan began practicing her four steps. Our pain cycle was so ingrained that I believed my job was to point out her shortcomings and make her start loving me better. When she spoke her four steps, I was at a loss. In our old dance, I knew her steps and mine. But once she started to dance the waltz, my rumba steps no longer fit. Oh, *I tried to pull her back into the rumba*, but she persisted in humility. Naturally my heart softened toward her. This invited me to examine myself. A humility shift by one partner dynamically invites the other partner to do the same. When both partners shift, grace begins to rain down on them. You'll witness softer responses, less escalating reactivity, and each will assume the best about the other. Emotional safety increases. (Later we'll share more about how long it may take for you to experience significant change.)

What do you do when your partner says, "What I know about me" or jumps right into saying their four steps? Breathe and calm down. Depending on the level of conflict you've had in your marriage and pain from the past, calming down is about all many of us can muster in the beginning. They may be trying to stop dancing the rumba, but for you, the rumba music is still playing. Manage the flood of emotion. Calm yourself; observe with curiosity how your partner is emotionally regulating. This may naturally soften your heart, unless your hurt and pain are so deep, so heavy, that moving toward them feels extremely risky. You may have, for example, given them multiple second chances only to be hurt again and again. Or there may have been a massive betrayal in your marriage, and one shift on their part (or a few) is not sufficient evidence of trustworthiness. Being guarded is understandable. Don't beat yourself up over this. Do what you can. For example, be curious about the idea that maybe, just maybe, they care about you. Or maybe acknowledge the effort: "I see you're trying." If words seem too much, try a small change of pace. Avoid yelling. Avoid criticizing. Avoid isolating. Avoid blaming. Avoid shaming yourself. Curb actions that you know perpetuate the pain, and shift away from pain and into peace, even if just a little.

When you are on the receiving end of your partner's humility shift, you must try to see how hard they are working to deal with the log in their own eye. With time you may come to appreciate it as an act of humility and love. Indeed, self-regulation is an act of love.

Eventually, most people will be able to feel loved by their partner when they take steps of humility. In the beginning, residual pain may make us doubt our partner's authenticity when they begin the four steps, and we may refuse to give them credit for the effort. Self-preservation stands in the way of receiving this act of love. But eventually, we can see that when our partner unpacks their four steps, they are choosing a level of self-discipline and utter vulnerability that is nothing short of an act of great love. Humility reveals a heart for God; that, too, is attractive and can foster a growing trust.

Valued by Nan and attracted to Nan is exactly what I felt the day she shared the following four steps with me. I was leaving on a business trip (there's that "travel" trigger again!) and was feeling late for my flight. I was already feeling anxious about it—*here we go again!*—feeling incompetent if I missed my flight, so when Nan asked to have a prayer with me before I ran out the door I snipped, "I'm not going to be late for my flight!," and I made her feel like I was blaming her for my being late (something I certainly did in the past). So, already in my pain (anxious about being late), I coped by making it her fault, and in so doing I triggered her pain. The last two minutes of our time together were filled with hurt feelings, angry looks, and emotional distance. We went from perfectly fine to perfectly isolated in nanoseconds.

When I returned the next day, Nan presented me with a handwritten note containing her four steps and a completely different attitude.

1. I felt unimportant.

2. I normally shut down, pull away emotionally, get angry, pout, and ruminate.

3. The truth is that I am loved and protected. You love me and want to pray with me.

4. I went to God to validate my worth. I'm staying in relationship with you (not pulling away). I thanked God for you while you were gone.

When I read those words, I felt disarmed. Grateful. Relieved. Open to her. Attracted to her. And *convicted*. Her humility invited me toward her...and to examine myself. This is how we grow.

Now let me point out something that is not in Nan's four steps. Early on when we were learning to say our four steps, she might have said something like, "And the truth is you were anxious." And though that would have been true, it's better not to point it out. Over time Nan has learned my self-imposed anxiety over being inadequate is strong. Because we have repeatedly talked through our four steps and she understands my pain very well, she knows I get anxious because I'm putting pressure on myself. She didn't mention it in her four steps because in the heat of dysregulation, using the word "you" might have triggered me even more. We suggest you avoid words that ignite the other and speak for yourself. Stick to your four steps.

REFINING THE PAIN STORY

I've grown in clarity about my own pain story as I've practiced being mindful. As I repeat the four steps and gain more insight into my family of origin and how I've carried things through the years, I understand it better. Sharing this understanding with Nan allows her to see my pain and have increasing compassion for it. In the beginning, my pain was a huge source of reactivity for our couple pain cycle (even though I didn't realize it). When I initially shared it, it made little sense to her; all she could see was my defensiveness and control—and it irritated her more. But once she began seeing my pain and having compassion for it, safety grew in our relationship. I felt more intimacy with her. I didn't have to hide my pain. I could trust her. That, in turn, helped me understand and share more fully.

"But Ron," one man said to me, "I don't want to see my wife's pain. I want her to see mine." Hearing your partner's first two steps can be hard, especially if you've felt neglected or insecure for a long time. In the beginning Nan didn't want to hear about my pain. After feeling unimportant and second to my career aspirations for years she wanted evidence that I cared for her. And that was understandable. But when she saw the effectiveness of this process and how it freed me up from old patterns, she leaned into self-regulating while I unpacked my steps. We were learning a whole new dance.

It starts with small changes in your typical pain cycle. Take just a step in that new dance. As you own your half of the cycle, anything you can do differently helps. As you manage your pain and alter your negative coping mechanisms, you'll see tiny changes. Remind yourself of the truth about your God-given identity and how you can respond in love.

Relatively healthy individuals in strong marriages might be able to make significant changes in their pain cycle quickly. Highly distressed couples, however, may find even small changes difficult. It may take some time to change things for good. The hardest work occurs in the beginning.

It took us quite a while before our largest relational gains were realized. Don't expect a miracle. Just start. Take small steps and trust the process.

CONFESSION

Responding with self-control and truth fosters peace. What's more, the confession involved in the four steps is very good for the soul. But it comes with risk. *Will I receive condemnation or compassion? Hurtful words or a hug?* Without a doubt, steps 1 and 2 are risky, but ironically, they are also life-giving. Choosing to own your frailties gives you the chance to let God affirm your worth and value long before you get it from your spouse. You can stop idolizing your spouse's approval, relying instead on what we like to call God-esteem, that is, the worth you carry as a result of being made in God's image and redeemed by the work of Christ. Confession and self-control, then, help each partner trust God instead of fragilely leaning on the other.

God is a God of peace, and he clearly wants us to experience his peace. The word "peace" occurs 345 times in scripture. The Spirit is literally life and peace. So set your mind on what the Spirit desires. Think about truth, put it into practice, and you will experience peace.

The four steps foster spiritual growth as well as usness. They help us love well in peace and pain. Centered in eternal truth, we can unpack emotional baggage, and love as Jesus loved—with a humble, sacrificial heart. Over time, this cultivates a new, more peaceful us. When spouses practice self-regulation...well, the sky's the limit.

IF YOU'RE IN A DIFFICULT MARRIAGE

The four steps work. If you're in a difficult marriage with a partner who shows no interest in working on the marriage, know that God cares for you and will not abandon you, even in your pain (*especially* in your pain). Keep yourself moving forward based on God's truth. Do not let pain dictate your actions. Pursue self-care, and emotional and physical safety for you and your children. Respond as best you can from a posture of peace. For example, you may say, "I want this marriage to work but I won't continue to subject myself to contempt. I'm going to take care of myself and the kids while you decide if you want to work on this with me." Manage you while they decide if they can manage themselves.

We always have a choice. Be empowered by truth. I mean, if you find yourself in prison in a foreign country, you can still self-regulate based on truth. If you find yourself all alone during the holidays, you can remind yourself of truth that empowers you to self-regulate. If your spouse isn't pulling their weight in the marriage, you can self-regulate, seek support, and prayerfully decide how to respond. The point is our circumstances and our pain do not get to dictate our response. Don't give situations or people in your life the power to override or control the truth about your identity and safety. So, move yourself into the four steps and trust you'll discover something helpful.

NEW SELF, PEACEFUL US CONVERSATION

- What do you imagine it would be like to say the four steps in front of each other? It may be comfortable when you're calm and in a good mood, but what would it be like to do when you're dysregulated?
- Can you agree that the phrase "What I know about me…" should be honored as a signal that someone is trying to manage their pain better? How will you respond when the other says it?
- What does calming down look like for you?
- Ironically, some people get really aggravated when their spouse begins to make changes to their pain cycle. What do you think you'll do?
- Say the four steps out loud with each other. Reference your pain cycle and peace cycle if necessary. Remember, steps 1–2 are from your pain cycle and steps 3–4 are from your peace cycle.

Even if only briefly, pray together about what you're learning and ask the Spirit's help in saying the four steps, especially when you're dysregulated.

CHAPTER 9

Practicing the Four Steps

At this point you've identified your pain story and how you tend to cope with predictable behaviors that keep you stuck. You've also learned that you're responsible for self-regulating and working on your side of your couple pain cycle or things won't improve. And you've learned to live in truth and behave differently based on that truth. Enter the four steps. They give you a tangible way to halt dysregulation and put on your more loving, emotionally safe new self. Humility and the four steps practiced regularly make for a mindful you and a peaceful *us*.

In this chapter, we'll share some pro tips about implementing the four steps and you'll discover how rehearsal (aka *practice*) rewires your brain—literally renewing your mind.

CHECK YOUR ASSUMPTIONS

Dysregulation that triggers survival mode sensations and activates emotional and bodily scanning for more threat is known as neuroception.[1] It recalibrates a person's baseline sense of safety. This can lead to perceived danger in moments or situations where it may or may not exist. In other words, pain makes us hypersensitive to more pain.

As Nan and I began restoring our marriage, my hypersensitivity to pain kept me alert for threat or injury even when there was none. The four steps helped me not overreact to inaccurate assumptions. Here's an example. I was in my home office one day working on a project. I usually turn my phone notifications off when I do that so I can focus. After a couple of hours, I saw that I had missed two calls from Nan. I was triggered in a millisecond. *She's probably so mad. For years she's complained that she can't get ahold of me when I'm working, and it makes her feel unimportant. This is not going to be good*, I thought.

I called her. My radar was up, scanning for conflict. She answered and seemed curt. The call ended quickly. *Yep, she's totally pissed.* Alarms were going off in my head concerning my safety and identity—and our usness.

About that time, Nan walked into our house and stuck her head in my office. No "Hello," just a quick glance, and she went directly into another room. *Yep, this is going to be a long night*, I told myself.

But then I paused and thought, *Exit Dysregulation Highway, Ron. Slow your roll. Check your assumptions. Manage your pain.* So, I took a few deep breaths to slow my heart rate and started working my four steps. What was I feeling? What do I usually do? Was there truth at work here that I had not considered? What should I do instead?

I decided to wait a few minutes before engaging Nan. I led by saying my four steps out loud. "[Step 1] After missing your calls, I felt inadequate and like a failure. [Step 2] I usually get defensive and find some crack in your feelings to blame you with. [Step 3] But the truth is, my value is set, even if you're upset. And I reminded myself that a lot is changing in us and in you, and I thought maybe I was wrong about my read on the whole situation...so, [Step 4] in order to stay connected I want to listen to how you are feeling about me not being available."

It turns out my assumptions were completely wrong. Every step of the way. Nan had been at Walgreens and called because she had a quick question to ask. Not connecting with me wasn't a big deal and she came home. When she walked in and bypassed my office, she wasn't angry; she was listening to a song through her earbuds (which I couldn't see) that spoke to her. She wanted to finish it and let me finish my project (a thoughtful consideration, I should add).

Now, in hindsight, it's understandable why I made those assumptions. In the past, anger is exactly what I could have expected from her in a situation like that, even if my unavailability was unavoidable. But here's the deal: your pain story doesn't know things are changing, and besides, it assumes the worst. You must slow it down. Speak aloud the four steps. It's a hopeful thing. Had I not done any of that, I would have made things ten times worse, I guarantee it.

Hypersensitivity doesn't have to dictate your reality. Let truth do that.

TAKING BABY STEPS TOWARD THE FOUR STEPS

Restoration Therapy has been life-changing for me and Nan. But given how entrenched our cycle was, that change didn't come quickly. Things might not change quickly for you either. Be gentle with yourself. Take baby steps.

Here's an example. While writing this book, we shared some of the pain and peace cycle concepts with a friend of ours. After Amy got home from our meeting, a conflict came up in her blended family marriage. This is what she said about her first attempt at applying what she had learned from us:

"When I realized I'd messed up, I felt shame and I wanted to control the mess I'd made. Instead of stoking that feeling, I observed it with curiosity. I noted, 'Shame is alerting me to my pain. It feels like I'm being chased by a bear, but there is no bear. So, what's the threat? Is my identity or safety under attack? Hmmmm. Oh! My identity as a competent parent—it feels like someone is trying to take that from me, perhaps rightly. But is that true? No. I am doing the best I can. Can I do better? Yes, so let me relax and put down my fists and put away my running shoes to see what there is to learn right now.'"

She then started self-regulating. In her words, she had to

turn off the "faucet of chemicals flooding my body" with self-regulating breath and by speaking truth. Once she was able to self-regulate, she had better clarity. After a little more reflection, she realized, "It's so good to learn that shame and blame have so little power. They're just signs saying, 'Pay attention to what you are believing in this moment.'"

That's a huge baby step, if you ask us. In the past, her feelings of inadequacy had a lot of power, neurologically speaking, and led her to the destructive coping behaviors of shame and blame. But now, she sees them for what they are—a signpost to pain that can be managed in other ways, bringing about a new self, new peace, and a new usness.

Even if you feel a little muddled with what you're learning and how to apply it, keep taking baby steps.

FIND YOUR RESOLVE

This last story raises another question: What if you're the only partner reaching for change? Kassandra was a divorced mother of two children when she met Julian. He was in his early forties. Julian had lived with a woman before but had never married. He didn't have any children when Kassandra and her kids came into his world. Because Kassandra had been deeply hurt by her first husband, who left her for another woman, she was eager to gain relationship skills that would guarantee her blended family marriage with Julian would not end in divorce. After learning about humility and the four steps, she began trying to implement them.

She worked to identify her pain and coping behaviors, then the peace cycle exercise to figure out how truth and new-self behaviors could open new responses from her. The first few occasions she said all four were awkward, and Julian was confused about what she was up to. But eventually it got easier, and she gained many insights into how sensitive she was to being hurt again. Ironically, she had to deal with a new hurt when trying to teach Julian what she was doing and why. She found hope in humility and wanted to share her insights with Julian, in part for his benefit, but also because sharing this growth path together would bring deeper trust and intimacy to their usness. Julian wasn't open to it. "I don't like self-help stuff," he said. "It's fine if you do it, but don't expect me to."

This poked her pain. *Sharply.* At first, she became dys-regulated, feeling anxious and fearful. *If Julian won't try, how can this marriage be any good? Do I not matter to him? Is this going to end like my first marriage?* But then she slowed her negative thinking and reflected again on what her experience of Julian seemed to confirm: *He is faithful. He is compassionate toward both me and my children. And he is committed to our marriage. Not being drawn into this "program" doesn't mean he doesn't love me. What I can do right now is emotionally-regulate myself and bring a better me to our relationship.* Essentially, Kassandra trusted that being intentional with her own journey of humility and working the steps might ultimately produce growth in their marriage. Indeed, we have witnessed many situations where this did happen (some, of course, do not). The resolve of one person can positively impact a marriage.

When both of you are working on humility and the four steps, change can be dramatic. Mario was a pastor of a large church in a metropolitan area. He was highly sought after by many members of his congregation and his days were full of meetings with people, hearing their stories of pain, and helping them connect in meaningful ways. He oversaw a large staff and had to deal with several issues every week involving staff-related concerns and ministry-related decisions. When he walked in the door each night, he wanted his wife, Elizabeth, to meet him with full attention and care, just as he had been giving his attention and care to others all day long. When she did not, he was hurt (feeling unwanted and insignificant) and would withdraw to the safety of isolation. He also carried painful feelings about their sexual relationship, as Elizabeth's desire for sex was not as high as his.

Elizabeth maintained a part-time accounting business while also balancing the needs and activities of their three children, who ranged in age from eleven to eighteen. She dreaded Mario walking in the door each evening; she knew that often she was too tired and too involved in trying to get dinner on the table and attending to their children to stop and give him the attention he desired. Frequently, she would force a warm and welcoming greeting to avoid Mario sulking through dinner. In her attempt to hide her true feelings, her resentment toward him grew deep. Her desire to be involved with him sexually diminished daily. Not wanting to connect with her husband tapped her pain story of not being good enough as a woman.

As Mario and Elizabeth came to understand their pain

and peace cycles, Elizabeth began to understand that pretending things were good (an act of performance) when Mario arrived home each evening was only contributing to her lack of desire to be with him. She began to understand that performing was destructive to their relationship as it caused her to want to withdraw and be alone. Mario learned that expecting his wife to give him her full attention each evening led him to be critical and demanding of her. And he finally came to see how that pressed her belief that she was less than adequate as a woman and wife, moving her further away from him.

And they also became intimately aware of the pain that drove these destructive coping behaviors. Mario's parents fought constantly when he was a child. The oldest of five, Mario essentially played the role of go-between for his parents so they wouldn't divorce and his siblings wouldn't reap the spillover hostility he did as a small child. He grew up learning how to coach and counsel others (a skill he aptly later applied to ministry). He believed his worth was in rescuing others. He longed for his parents—and now his wife—to take the initiative to care for him.

In exploring her pain cycle, Elizabeth realized that she withdrew from trusting herself to her husband to avoid the pain of being rejected. Throughout her life, vulnerability and pursuing family members who were difficult to love only left her feeling unwanted and frustrated. As a result, she learned to temper her desire for connection and withdraw as soon as tension arose.

Mario connected to the truth that he had value even when his wife was not fully attentive to him. That helped him self-soothe when he came home. He could help with all that was going on in the house with dinner and their children and spend time investing in them rather than being critical. As Elizabeth began to live in the truth that she was enough and valued in her roles as a wife, mother, and part-time employee, she began to stay engaged with her husband (even when he seemed preoccupied) and be vulnerable with him. As the couple learned how to partner as a team with their work schedules, home responsibilities, and parenting, their love for each other took on a new dimension of openness and vulnerability. Those new feelings of partnership, honesty, and companionship eventually refreshed their sexual relationship.

Not all change comes quickly. Find your resolve. Begin working your four steps—take whatever baby step is in front of you today—and trust that with time and practice, new experiences and new patterns will emerge within your marriage.

SEEK PEACE AND PURSUE IT: PRACTICE, PRACTICE, PRACTICE

In the first few verses of 1 Peter 3, Peter offers some words of advice first to wives, then to husbands. Then, he says to both, "Finally, all of you, have unity of mind, sympathy, brotherly love, a tender heart, and a humble mind. Do not repay evil for evil or reviling for reviling, but on the contrary, bless, for to this you were called, that you may obtain a blessing. For

'Whoever desires to love life
and see good days,
let him keep his tongue from evil
and his lips from speaking deceit;
let him turn away from evil and do good;
let him seek peace and pursue it'" (1 Pet. 3:8–11 ESV)

Loving well begins with humility, unity, and a tender heart. When conflict occurs, loving well means not responding to mistreatment with further harm, but with a blessing. Hold your tongue, watch what you say, and do good to the other. But how? How can we be that self-controlled? Humility and the four steps are designed to get you there.

Seek peace and pursue it. Peace is what we're after; it takes active pursuit. This same principle is repeated by the apostle Paul in 1 Corinthians 14:1. It's likely you know what the preceding chapter is about. First Corinthians 13 is one of the greatest treatises on love ever written. It's in most weddings and is referenced frequently in sermons. But what are the first few words of chapter 14? One translation says, "Let love be your highest goal!" (NLT). Another emphatically says, "Pursue love…" (ESV). Paul has just defined what it means to love, and now he says, "Go get it with everything you have." The word "pursue" here is not passive; it does not mean mosey over and see if you can find love. It means *strive for it with intense effort*; run after it; chase it down.[2]

To become a mature, loving person, you need intention. Go after love with everything you've got. People who expect an intimate marriage without any effort of their own will be extremely disappointed. Know yourself and your emotional triggers, learn self-control, and respond from truth instead of reacting out of pain. In other words, *seek peace and pursue it* with your whole heart. You've gained many insights about yourself so far in this book. Put it into practice. Like learning any new skill, loving well takes practice, practice, practice.

Earlier we mentioned the brain's ability to rewire neuropathways (neuroplasticity) which reduces old-self reactivity. Practice rewires neurons literally renewing the mind. Practicing your four steps makes new responses stronger and more familiar to the brain. Imagine trying to brush your teeth with the opposite hand. New things can make us feel clumsy and frustrated. It takes focus and intention to do something routine in a new way. However, if you continue to practice, eventually the behavior becomes familiar because neuroplasticity allows the brain to develop new synaptic and neuronal connections.[3] Self-control and putting on new behaviors that are more loving requires intentional practice and repetition. Over time what at first felt frustrating will be automatic.

How much time? Our clinical experience suggests that most people need to repeat the four steps while in a mild-to-moderate state of dysregulation around fifty times. For a while, you're still brushing left-handed.

Previously we suggested you take a picture of your pain and peace cycles to keep them with you. You're beginning to put words on wounds throughout your life to your identity and sense of emotional safety. These realities impact daily behavior in nanoseconds at the neurological level, yet rarely do we acknowledge them at a conscious level. Become familiar with your own pain. Learn to recognize what triggers your pain. You may need to refer to the picture of your pain cycle and your peace cycle often. Keep at it. The more you implement the four steps when triggered, the better.

Practice your four steps in calm moments, too. Speaking them in calm, regulated moments is easier than when you are dysregulated and in pain. That's why it's helpful in the beginning to practice when you don't need it. Go through the motions so your brain can begin to form new neurological ruts that you can go to easily when you're dysregulated. Practice saying them when alone and practice them as a couple. At first Nan and I said them in a light and humorous tone. The ruts of our couple pain cycle were very deep; we came to expect certain negative things from each other to the point that we each acted like the other had already said or done them even when they hadn't! It helped to hear ourselves and one another in a different light in preparation for when conflicts arose later.

Practice calming yourself. When you feel yourself beginning to get agitated, anxious, or upset with a coworker, or when you have a financial strain, a stressful situation with your parent(s) or sibling(s), or a toddler—whatever the trigger—use it as an opportunity to calm down. Practice activating that direct connection between slowing your breathing and heart rate, and lowering your blood pressure to bring your prefrontal cortex—and best loving behavior—back online.

Pro Tip: When dysregulated, you can begin slowing your heart rate and calming down by focusing on your breathing. This is the one physiological aspect of dysregulation that we can control. Slowing your breathing sends a powerful neurological signal to your brain and body that you want to calm down. Deep and slow exhalations are key to this process.[4]

Finally, practice the four steps when one of you gets dysregulated. It doesn't matter who started it or who is more distressed. Just start working *your* steps. Each time you do—even if you fumble your way through—you make renewing your mind a reality.

Nicholas and Jessica had been married for two years when they came to therapy. A blended family couple with five children, Nicholas "blew up" nearly every time Jessica talked to her ex-husband. "She accommodates to him all the time," he explained. "But my opinion isn't worth much ever. Honestly, I think she would still rather be married to him." Remarks like that led Jessica to retreat and hide her co-parent conversations from Nicholas for fear that he would get mad. But that, too, infuriated Nicholas. He got angrier and more resentful, and she got more distant and self-protective.

The breakthrough came when they began managing their pain differently through the four steps. Nicholas put the pieces together when he said, "What I know about me is that I feel [step 1] unimportant and insecure. When I feel this way [step 2] I get angry, intimidating, and resentful. But the truth is [step 3] you cherish me and your kids. You try to do right by your kids—and that sometimes means having to flex with your ex to make their world less stressful. I can see how difficult that is to balance, all while trying to honor me and our marriage. And so [step 4], I'm talking myself through this moment. I feel the stress rising, but I'm going to hear you out, try not to make harsh judgments, and try to help you navigate these tough decisions."

In pleasant surprise, Jessica just about fell on the floor. This was so different—and so relieving. She could lean into Nicholas. He was trying to be there for her—which helped her trust him with her dilemmas. She responded, "Thank you for that. I see how hard you are working on this—and that you love me. I'm feeling alone in this [step 1] and that triggers my pain from being abandoned in my first marriage. I want to trust you with this stuff, but what I usually do is hide it from you [step 2] and resent that I can't talk to you about it. The truth is [step 3] you love me and the kids. So, I'm choosing [step 4] to be more honest with you about things that come up with my ex and to trust that we can work through it. Honestly, if you were to hear me out and not assume he's more important to me than you are, it would help me share more of my frustrations with you—my ex really drives me crazy sometimes, but we never get to that because I'm defending myself from feeling attacked. I want to share this stuff with you, so thank you for saying you're going to give me the benefit of the doubt."

Can you hear a new usness being formed?

Here's the bottom line: practice when you're not upset and practice when you are.

PRACTICE IN MICROPAIN MOMENTS

The minor irritations of everyday life can become major opportunities for growth, but most of us skip right over them. At least once a week Josh found himself cussing out a driver on the freeway. Someone would shift into his lane or drive slower than the freeway flow, and out of nowhere his heart rate would jump and his blood pressure rocket upward, and he'd yell at the other driver as if they could hear him. But did he ever wonder what this micropain moment was telling him about himself?

Thomas is a 3 on the Enneagram. He plans his day so he can be successful and efficient so others will think well of him. Does he do this because he's a 3? Or maybe he's a 3 because pain has created an insecurity in him, and he copes by proving his worth every single day. Either way, "I'm a 3" doesn't help him face his fear.

Consuela hates being cold. If she's with friends in a cold restaurant she'll complain constantly or leave early, even if everyone is excited to be together. No big deal, right? Or maybe escaping these moments is about feeling emotionally cold, and this pain and coping is trying to teach her something.

In our parental journey we've discovered that common aggravating parenting moments are often dripping with a pain story behind them that has nothing to do with our child. Sure, your child misbehaved, but my strong reaction usually has more to do with my pain than their behavior. I learned early in our kids' lives that a fiery reaction from me toward one of our children who acted out at church was more about my identity than their behavior. I wanted people to think I was a good parent; again, my need to gain approval and have others view me as capable was the core pain that led me to react harshly.

Here's another one. If you're like me, you have a love-hate relationship with air travel. You love the modern marvel that allows you to hop on a plane and arrive in another city or country within just a few hours. But when it comes to a screeching halt because of the weather or some unforeseen maintenance issue, you hate being stuck in Timbuktu. For years I traveled with anxiety over what *might* go wrong. And when it did, if my wife was traveling with me, I let my irritability and efforts to retake control ripple on to her. After all, my prickliness was justified (at least, that's what my pain was telling me).

Then one day I asked myself, "Ron, what is going on with you? When you fly you get controlling and bossy and are a real pain to be around. Chase the pain, Ron. Chase your pain. What's behind the anxiety and control?"

That simple question—though now obvious because of what I've already shared throughout this book—opened the door to insight and change. Chasing your pain puts words on what is driving your poor coping, and it helps you decide if you want to remain a victim of it. But here's the deal: Unfortunately, most people live their whole lives not knowing why they fret over little things. They never see opportunity in the pain.

Larry's boss never explicitly said that he expects Larry to reply to texts after business hours, yet Larry always did. Even if it meant interrupting family time with his kids. His wife complained that he let his phone steal him away from their children. He agreed in principle, but he wouldn't put his phone in "do not disturb" mode, and when a message came in, he dealt with it immediately. After attending one of our Mindful Marriage conferences, Larry took a simple step of humility and began to ask himself, "Dude, what's the big deal?" Chasing his pain made him realize he was anxious.

"Anxious about what?" he asked himself. "It's probably related to your sense of identity or feeling emotionally safe. Put words on it."

"Well, I guess I'm concerned my boss won't think well of me if I don't work when she works."

"Why is that?"

"I don't know. My high school baseball coach always said, 'You've got to give a hundred and ten percent if you want to get ahead in this world.'"

He kept wrestling with it until he could summarize what he was discovering about himself. "So, if you don't reply to the text, you'll never get a raise, and your coach will be disappointed in you."

"No way," he said to himself. "That's not true. And even if it was, that's lame. And there's no way that little fear has been making me ignore my wife and kids all this time."

See, that's the thing. It likely is. In part because it really isn't "little" at all. As Larry continues to unpack this, he may find that the disappointment he felt from his coach has created a hypersensitivity to feeling that pain again. He'll do anything to avoid it, even if the disappointment is just in his imagination. And if Larry is courageous to humbly articulate this pain to his wife, he may notice many other micromoments when his actions are compelled by the same pain.

"What's the truth?" Larry finally asked himself (step 3). "Well, first, my coach doesn't get to decide if I'm worthwhile or not. Jesus settled that on the cross. Secondly, not responding to a text might cost me my bosses momentary admiration and my coach's approval. But are either of those things more valuable than being fully present in my children's lives? And what if my unavailability to my kids sends a message that they aren't good enough for me? I wouldn't want that."

(Step 4) *So, Larry, what are you going to do differently instead?* Well, first, I'm going to share my pain cycle with my wife and ask her to pray for me as I try to recognize its power in my life and step out from under it. And then I'm going to tell my boss that if she needs a quick response from me, I need her to call me (that will signal that it's an emergency), but otherwise, I'd prefer not to reply to messages till the next business day and I'm hoping she's okay with that. If she's curious why this is happening, I'll find the courage to tell her about my pain and peace cycles. Who knows, maybe she has some pain that is driving her one-hundred-and-ten-percent belief system, too."

Let the micropain moments of life lead you to a better

understanding of your pain story and help you to practice the four steps.

WHEN THE FOUR STEPS ARE NOT ENOUGH

Every person has a pain cycle. We want to clarify at this point that being in your peace cycle does not mean that you will not feel pain. It means that you will respond to painful and difficult situations in a more constructive manner. We believe that knowing your pain and peace cycles will help you think clearer and make better decisions about the challenges ahead. Let's now consider the limitations of the pain-and-peace-cycles approach to more extreme marital situations.

As we said, the four steps are not designed to fix your spouse. At times people are drawn to this strategy because they are hoping they can change their spouse, thereby fixing the relationship. The four steps are not another control tactic. Honestly, to view your partner as the problem is prideful; believing you know what's best, you will contend with your partner. Humility is contending with yourself. Focus on self-regulation, not other-regulation.

Now, having said that, what if you are taking an honest look at yourself, but your spouse is not, or seems deeply stuck in harmful or chaotic behavior? What role do the four steps play in your marriage then?

If you are in an abusive relationship, please do not hear us saying, "Stay in your lane and stay in an unsafe relationship."

Rather, get help. Work with a therapist to, at a minimum, learn the truth of your worth and value separate and apart from this destructive relationship, and make a plan to find safety for yourself and your children. Research tells us that it takes approximately seven times for someone to leave an abusive relationship. If you're in an abusive relationship, create an exit plan. Without a plan many people return to domestic abuse situations due to a lack of money, no place to live, or an inadequate support system. To develop a plan that is going to be successful, a person needs to know the truth of who they are and be able to think through the plan in a logical, meaningful way.

Jada's husband, Carter, struggled off and on with alcohol. At best, he had an occasional social drink when they went out; at worst, during stressful seasons of life he drank regularly to the point of impairment. Jada sought help during one of those seasons and learned the four steps. She also learned that sharing her steps outwardly when Carter was drunk became ammunition that would be fired back at her later. Jada couldn't make Carter self-regulate, even when he was sober, and she couldn't expect him to appreciate her efforts to manage herself better, either. Until something shifted in Carter, she would need to work her side of the pain and peace cycles in isolation.

Living with an addict can cause feelings of inadequacy (*if I were enough, they wouldn't drink*), powerlessness (*there is nothing I can do to change this situation*), being unloved (*if they loved me enough, they would stop*), and many other lies we tell ourselves about the relationship. In believing those lies we might step into the destructive behavior of helping our partners hide their addictions, getting angry, or isolating ourselves from others. If you are the spouse of an addict, the path for healing is the pain and peace cycles, learning the truth about who you are apart from the addict, and learning how to respond to their chaotic behavior in a healthy way.

Steve's wife was extremely critical of him—contemptuous, some would say. Amanda berated him every chance she got. For years he put up with it. Every time Amanda criticized him, she confirmed what his mother always said about him, and what he believed about himself—that he was a poor version of a man. When Steve began working his four steps, he realized the lie he held for so long and began to replace it with the truth of his worth in Christ Jesus. But how should he now respond to his wife's criticism? He never liked it before, but he did think he deserved it, so he took it. Now, he wanted to fight back with every bone in his body.

Some people fear that telling partners in verbally abusive situations like Steve's to focus less on their partner's behavior and more on their part of the marital dance will make them more susceptible to abuse. Self-regulation makes you *less* susceptible to harsh or manipulative behavior. Self-controlled people can create and enforce healthy boundaries. Steve learned, for example, that he didn't have to shut up and take it, but neither did he have to counterattack his wife or make her stop saying such things (both of which would likely just escalate their negativity). On one occasion when Amanda made a cutting remark Steve said, "That really hurts. And usually, I just sit here and take it, but I'm not going to because I'm worth better. I won't argue with you, but I won't subject myself to that, either. Stop talking to me that way. It hurts. I need to take a walk and step away for a little while, but I'll be back because you're important to me."

Can you see all four steps? Steve acknowledges the pain, states what he usually does, roots himself in his eternal identity (truth), and chooses healthy behaviors. The whole statement is bathed in gentleness and self-respect—and it powerfully declares that he isn't her helpless victim anymore. What he doesn't do is wait on her to coregulate his value in the marriage; instead, he takes charge of his value and is empowered to honor that value.

How she responds to this is yet to be seen; our guess is she will belittle his statement with more criticism. But eventually, his ongoing refusal to subject himself to her contempt will upset the status quo and invite their usness to evolve—which might result, we should add, in him moving out so he isn't subjected further to her abuse. Perhaps him moving out will finally wake her up. Perhaps not. Hopefully it won't come to that.

Practicing RT isn't a silver bullet to fix every marriage. It takes two to tango, as the old saying goes. When addictive behavior is a factor, seek support and/or intervention from a community of friends or family, your church, or a 12-step program. Nan, for instance, benefited from the 12-step program re:generation[5] which dramatically impacted her life and our usness; now she leads groups of other people seeking sobriety. (By the way, the 12-steps also foster humility and change in people, just in a different way, but it can be just as dramatic.) The legal system may be necessary when abuse is involved because it won't let a partner harm or intimidate the other.

And in all these situations, go to the Father in earnest prayer. For example, when one highly motivated partner who is actively working on themselves feels helpless in their relationship with a chronically depressed or unmotivated partner, we suggest they pray that the Lord will take their partner to the end of themselves—through whatever means necessary. Unfortunately, hitting bottom is a necessary pain that wakes some people up (but not all). It's ugly to watch, for sure, but without God's opposition, some people never find humility.

And while you wait for the Lord to move through these resources in the life of your spouse, stay in your lane. Work on repenting of your worldly desires (see James 4:3–4) and managing your pain cycle differently. Taking off your old self—especially when your spouse is still living in theirs— putting on your new self, and trusting God with what you cannot control, is your best next step.

LITTLE BY LITTLE, STEP BY STEP

While writing this book, I had total knee replacement surgery on my left knee. I've had other surgeries and medical procedures through the years, but the post-op pain with this one far exceeded them all. And physical therapy wasn't much fun either.

One of the initial goals of physical therapy with this type

of surgery is to get your flexibility back within the first two weeks. Flexibility must precede strengthening, because if you don't regain your range of motion, you won't be able to walk correctly let alone run, lay down, or do lots of things. So, your first two goals are to extend your leg straight at 0° and bend it to an angle of 120°.

I was put on a machine that sat on my bed and for six hours a day would bend my knee back and forth. Initially, it was set at 60°. My physical therapist, Mike, instructed me to increase the bend 5° each day. That doesn't sound like much, but believe me, every degree of change was painful. Without fail, every single day I had to fight discouragement, because what I discovered is that whatever gains I had made the previous day I had to back up 15° to start the next day. For example, on the third day I worked up to 75°. But on day four, even though my goal was 80°, I had to back up to 60° and slowly work my way back to what I had achieved the day before. And even then, it hurt, pulled muscles in my thigh, and basically made me feel like I had made no progress at all.

At least that was what my pain was saying to me. Every single day I had to fight the thought that I wasn't doing this right or that I had lost whatever gains I had made the previous day. And in rejecting the lies of my pain and continuing to practice my therapy exercises, what I learned over time is that trusting the process, which included backing up sometimes, and acting on the truth my therapist repeated ("You will get better if you keep doing the exercises."), produced more gain than loss. Here's how it would go: within the first forty-five minutes I could warm up to the previous day's goal and then pursue my new daily goal. Remember, I had six hours on the machine per day! In the remaining time I could hit the next new goal! That process happened every single day for the three weeks they had me on the machine. What felt like regression to start the day was a strategic way of getting better.

You will have moments while implementing the four steps when you feel like you've accomplished something monumental. You see the difference, you feel the difference, your relationship experiences the difference, and you will celebrate hitting your goal. And then, in the next moment or the next day, you will feel like you've lost everything you gained. This is not true; what is true is that you must be patient with yourself as you practice and repractice what you have already learned. Living out your new self does not come as second nature for quite some time. But you are making progress, little by little, step-by-step.

NEW SELF, PEACEFUL US CONVERSATION:

- Since pain makes us hypersensitive to more pain, why is it important to check our assumptions before letting them dysregulate us?
- Could you relate to any of the people in the stories in this chapter? What do you have in common?
- How are you doing so far at taking baby steps toward the four steps?
- It is *practice* that rewires neurons within the brain and quite literally renews the mind, transforming us into

a living sacrifice, holy and acceptable to God (Rom. 12:1–2). Practice makes our new responses stronger and more familiar to the brain. When do you practice the four steps? (Remember, practice both when you're *not* dysregulated and when you are.)

- When abuse or costly addiction is present, couples need outside intervention. Are you in need of that?

CHAPTER 10

Peace for the Journey

The four steps help you cooperate with the sanctifying work of the Holy Spirit. But like all change strategies, wisdom is needed to apply it to specific circumstances. In the last chapter, for example, Nicholas and Jessica's pain cycle was triggered in part by their ongoing interaction with her former spouse. Marital pain cycles being activated by a third person is a common dynamic in stepcouples. The conflict in many blended family couples has as much to do with their past (e.g., former spouses, former in-laws, first family traditions) as their present (e.g., stepparent-stepchild conflict, parenting dilemmas, and estate planning). Where children fit within the marriage and how spouses interact as parent and stepparent are as predictive of couple conflict as how they communicate together.[1]

In this chapter we'll address some common marital contexts that impact how couples implement the four steps and make some observations about living them out that may make your journey more efficient. In other words, know the ocean in which you swim.

MURKY WATERS: BLENDED FAMILIES

Couples in stepfamilies swim in a different ocean, if you will, than couples in first marriages.[2] The stepfamily ocean has a cooler relational water temperature; most everyone has experienced a significant loss that acts as a strong undercurrent, often moving stepfamily members away from one another (instead of toward). Blended families also experience a few more sharks; ex-spouses, co-parenting issues, and the stress of integrating are common examples. And another thing: The water is less clear. Stepfamily life is murky in the beginning (and therefore ripe for conflict), roles are unclear (what is a stepparent supposed to do, anyway?), rituals and traditions are hazy, and relationships lack clear definition.

To help couples navigate this ocean well I have produced a series of books like *The Smart Stepfamily* and *Building Love Together in Blended Families* (the latter coauthored with Dr. Gary Chapman) and founded a ministry that produces a podcast, livestreams, video curriculum, online resources— and trains church leaders in the principles of stepfamily ministry. Exploring the principles of those resources is beyond the scope of this book. Suffice it here to say that blended family couples must get stepfamily smart to navigate this ocean well.

Each person within a blended family (and this includes former spouses, stepsiblings, stepgrandparents, etc., etc.) has a pain cycle that often intersects with multiple other pain cycles. Throughout this book, for example, we've focused on how husband and wife pain cycles intersect, creating a couple pain cycle. But we can have pain cycles in many relationships. In a stepfamily, for instance, a husband might bring his individual pain cycle to bear on his co-parenting relationship with his former wife. (We don't have different pain cycles for different people.) And she will express her reactivity with him. That co-parenting pain cycle we might call it, then, potentially intersects (collides) with his marital pain cycle. Even further, his three children all have individual pain cycles. Their pain might be, for example, due to feeling unsafe in their parents' conflictual home before the divorce and the ongoing hostility that continues after the divorce. Each child will cope in their own way. One child might, for example, escape into their social network at school, while another tries to control how the parents interact. Still the third might blame the stepmom for everything that has happened. There are intersecting pain cycles here between husband and ex-wife, dad and son, husband and new wife, stepdaughter and stepmother. It's a complex mix of coping responses.

It's not necessary to map all those relationships and individual pain cycles (though it might be insightful to do so). Just manage yourself within each relationship. Work your four steps and find self-regulation no matter who you are interacting with. Self-regulation is what you can contribute to every relationship. This is particularly helpful to children. What every dysregulated child needs is a self-regulating adult. You show them how to self-regulate by example. In addition, some children will be open, at some point in their life, to you walking them through the exercises in this book. Mapping their pain and peace cycles can be as beneficial for them as it has been for you.[3]

NEW HORIZONS: DATING COUPLES

Couples who are falling in love tend to see nothing but beautiful sand and water while failing to notice the rip current that is sometimes present just a few feet offshore. Dating couples have a natural blindness to pain in themselves and their partners, and to yellow flashing lights—or even red lights—about the health of their partner or relationship. Infatuation and rose-colored glasses seemingly cover a multitude of sins, when what both partners really need to do is get honest about their pain story and the developing patterns in their usness. Dating or engaged couples cannot be discerning about the pace of their relationship or the prognosis for their relationship if they can't see what is pushing them together.

Cohabiting before marriage is a good example of this blindness. For example, the pain of being alone or the fear of getting into a marriage that fails drives many people into cohabiting relationships, despite a wealth of research indicating that couples who cohabit before making a strong commitment to marriage and to one another have *more* relationship distress and *more* difficulty in being objective about the quality of their relationship than non-cohabiting dating couples.[4] Ironically, the pain they are trying to avoid by cohabiting is more likely. These findings affirm God's protection and provision for our good. His boundary around sex before marriage is trying to protect people from blindly enveloping themselves into an unhealthy relationship. And if children are brought or born to this less than permanent home, the family instability works against their emotional development and maturation process. God wants to protect them as well. Here's the point: unrecognized pain can easily drive dating couples to ignore God's loving protection and live together long before it serves their relationship. If this is your season of life, strive to stay objective about your relationship and pay attention to any internal pain or fear that is diluting your objectivity. And explore your pain cycle and the story behind it. Doing that work now will help you to be more discerning about a partner and decisions about marriage. Pain, like pride, blinds us. Becoming more emotionally healthy and self-regulated will protect you from poor relationship discernment.

UNDERCURRENTS: YOUNG CHILDREN, TEENS, EMPTY NESTS

Parenting brings many transitions—most of them are wanted, a few are not. Nearly all of them can trigger you. After all, we are desperate for our children's well-being and want to love and care for them in a trustworthy manner—which we don't always do. Every season of parenting brings dilemmas you didn't see coming and issues that can easily divide you. At one point Nan and I had three children under the age of five. For a few years we didn't get much sleep, much less find time to nurture our usness. Other couples have combinations of biological children and adopted or foster children. Identity issues (relative to belonging and worth) are common in adopted and fostered children, and their interactions with biological children in the home over time vary from fantastic to rejecting. The dangers in these oceans, ironically, are usually chosen. Nevertheless, they are dangerous.

And then there are the adolescent years and the ensuing transition to adult children. Adolescence, even in the healthiest homes, often brings conflict between parent and child, or between parents when they disagree on how to deal with the child's strivings for independence. Boundary questions abound about kids and smartphones, social media, friendships, choice of college and expense, etc., etc. Nan and I have often said that our sons lost their ever-lovin' minds when they hit their late teens. We had periods of high conflict, anger, frustration, and anxiety over the direction of their lives. Thankfully, the rough waters subsided after a few years, and we started to like them again. (We never stopped loving them, but we sure didn't like them for a while!) The good news is that resources for these predictable seasons of life are readily available. Equip yourself to understand the ocean in which you swim and guard your marriage by building your parental plan and finding unity. The next chapter will say a few things about applying the four steps in parenting.

ROUGH SEAS: SEASONS OF DIFFICULTY

A marriage of any length of time will undoubtedly experience seasons of difficulty. External tsunamis that attack your marriage or family include things like financial stress, devastating circumstances to your possessions or home (e.g., tornado, fire, or flooding), social injustice and mistreatment, caring for a special-needs child, chronic illness, concerns for adult children or aging parents,[5] and end-of-life challenges. The amount of stress and heartache that such things can bring requires constant work and attention to how it is impacting your marriage.

We mentioned earlier that Nan and I lost our middle son, Connor, to an MRSA staph infection in February 2009. Connor was twelve. His older brother, Braden, was fourteen, and our youngest son, Brennan, was ten at the time. We have written and spoken many times about this shattering event and how much it has recalibrated our life and marriage. And since we know that grief is a journey, not a destination, we believe that we will continue to walk out our grief as long as we live.[6]

In the beginning, we both were completely devastated. How does one attune to a spouse when your chest feels like an elephant is sitting on it? How does someone feel sexual desire when even their skin aches and you can't stop crying? How do you talk about what you now consider to be pointless and temporal subjects when death and eternity are the only subjects that matter? Obviously, you can't. And, yet, even amid our grief, we fought to find grace for each other, to give each other space to grieve as needed, and to connect in whatever ways possible. Over time, as we learned to carry our grief, the more regular rhythms of our marriage returned—but that was not until Nan dealt with a coping dependency on alcohol and prescription medication that developed during the first decade after Connor's death. This brings us to another type of difficulty: internal issues that develop within a marriage.

If external tsunami waves pummel your marriage from the outside, internal hurricanes can also wreak havoc on the support systems and resources available to your marriage, and ultimately, your marital peace. Nan coped, in part, with Connor's death by numbing herself with alcohol and prescription medications. After hitting bottom and crying out to God, in what we describe as nothing less than a miraculous moment of God's intervention, Nan faced her coping behavior and sought help. Early in our marriage I had brought a hurricane of pain and distrust when my coping pattern of performance and perfectionism at work led me to emotionally abandon Nan, and now she had lost my trust. She sought help from the 12-step ministry re:generation. And together we again turned to the four steps as we began rebuilding our usness (see the next section on rebuilding trust).

Perhaps you have or are swimming in an ocean that is experiencing the hurricanes of infidelity, porn addiction, excessive spending or eating, and physical, verbal, or emotional abuse. Seek outside help. The four steps provide the backbone for rebuilding your relationship in these situations, but most couples who have experienced significant violations of trust and emotional safety need a competent guide to help them stay afloat in these raging seas. RT therapists and many other competent counselors are available to support your efforts to rebuild and restore your relationship.[7] Nan and I are a good example of what it can do for your marriage.

DAMAGED SHIPS: REBUILDING TRUST

Rebuilding after trust violations is difficult. Major violations like abuse, infidelity, or addiction top this list, but lying, patterns of emotional unavailability, siding with a child against your spouse, even prioritizing your smartphone over focused attention to your spouse impacts marital safety and connectedness. More than one-third of married Americans (37 percent) say that their spouse is often on the phone or some kind of screen when they would prefer to talk or do something together as a couple. And it's worse for younger couples. A full 44 percent of married adults under age thirty-five say that their spouse is on the phone too much, compared with 34 percent of those aged thirty-five to fifty-five.[8] But why does it matter? Because turning to your phone means turning away from your spouse. It's a micromoment that says, *This is more important than you.* The first time it happens may not be the end of the world, but a repetitive pattern of turning away erodes trust and safety. For couples already in distress, the smartphone becomes a convenient way to avoid problems. The point is this: anything that has become a third party in your usness needs focused attention, repair, and discipline to get rid of it and overcome how it has hurt your relationship.

Begin by identifying your pain and peace cycles and working the four steps. Identifying your individual pain cycles, including what you're currently doing with your pain, is critical to getting a handle on what's currently happening. The peace cycle gives you a target to work toward. But when trust has been fractured, the following guardrails will help you move toward peace.

First, both partners must acknowledge that you have experienced something that has disseminated trust in your usness. There is hope to rebuild your relationship, but you must acknowledge the seriousness of what has happened and your part in it. Trust is further eroded if the wounding partner minimizes their behavior or tries to rush the offended partner back into trust.

Todd discovered that his wife, Jennifer, was sending flirtatious texts to a coworker. Not just once, but multiple times. Jennifer pushed back: "I never slept with him or even spent time with him outside of work. This is no big deal." This revealed how disconnected she was to her vows and to Todd's feelings—and things just got worse. The process toward forgiveness and rebuilding trust begins with an honest acknowledgment of what has happened, followed by an expressed desire to stop the offensive behavior and rebuild the relationship. The scriptures simply call this confession. And without it—and a commitment to permanently turn away from that behavior (repentance)—reconciliation will be impossible.

Rebuilding after a significant betrayal (e.g., infidelity, multiple violations of trust) will take lots of time. Recovery from infidelity at a minimum takes a couple of years, if not many years. That's a very long road, which is why a firm commitment to restore the relationship must be articulated by both partners. If an active chemical or porn addiction, for example, contributed to the broken trust, pursuing sobriety is necessary. There is no way to restore trust if the addictive behavior continues.

A temptation for the offending partner is to confess their part *while blaming*. It sounds like, "I confess I did that but only because you've hurt me for years. When are you going to face up to that?" Here's the thing: the betraying partner usually has legitimate complaints that need to be addressed *eventually*, but at the beginning of recovery, you must stay in the hot seat for the major violation you committed. Your betrayal dwarfs your complaints. Your behavior has cost you the privilege of diverting attention to your spouse's behavior. Besides, your behavior is your responsibility, not theirs. Likely they have things they eventually need to own and confess, but you're still responsible for your actions. In other words, stay in a humble posture. Face the music—again and again. Confession is an act of humility—and sometimes it gets hard remaining in that posture and facing your partner's anger. But there you must remain.

And while you're there, do the hard work of examining why you did what you did. Your pain cycle should help reveal this to you. For example, for many people who betray their partner it comes down to this: turning to porn or another person is coping behavior (escape) meant to alleviate pain in your sense of worth. You turned to someone or something other than God to distract you from the pain of feeling unloved. In other words, affairs are easy fixes to otherwise hard challenges. You see, ultimately, you didn't manage your pain well and the coping behavior you turned to has violated trust and now is the focal point of pain for your marriage. Digging into your pain cycle will reveal all of that.

Now turn to the truth. You were looking to the wrong source for your value; it can't come from the created, it must come from the Creator. And when you're disappointed in not being able to connect with your partner sexually, the truth is you're still valuable because of Christ, and the truth is you don't have to turn to "easy" because the Holy Spirit can provide strength to endure your pain and manage it a different way. You don't have to lose your integrity every time your spouse doesn't show up for you in the way you desire. Turn away from "easy" and turn toward the good. This, by the way, is what your spouse must see for trust to be rebuilt over time. They need to see a repentant, contrite you who is striving for change—and walking it out day after day after day. You must become trustworthy. Then and only then might their heart soften toward you.

And now a word to the offended partner. You have been hurt and you have the right to speak of your pain. When Jesus instructs his disciples in Matthew 18:15–20 in how to handle personal offenses, he specifically tells the wounded person to tell the offending person his fault. That is the first step on the road to reconciliation. The second step is your spouse owning their fault, confessing it, repenting, and seeking forgiveness. The third step is you granting forgiveness. And the fourth is both of you rebuilding trust over time. Depending on the size of the offense, this process can take a very long time. To fix the marriage quickly, some people minimize their own pain and skip to "Everything's okay." It's not. And an artificial healing process won't create lasting trust. But in the same vein, you can't get stuck at step one. You may spend a few months telling them their fault, asking questions about why the affair, for example, happened and what they were thinking while having it. Those are appropriate questions for a season. But eventually, *assuming your spouse has confessed their wrongdoing, repented, and is striving to walk a new path of trustworthiness*, you'll need to shift your heart first in the direction of forgiveness and then, if your partner continues to prove their commitment to repentance, toward incremental trust.

Notice that forgiveness and trust are separate. One reason betrayed spouses refuse to forgive is that they think it requires trust. That's not the case. You can forgive an employee for robbing your bank and still never put them in charge of the vault again. Restoring trust after a significant betrayal will not happen unless the offending partner truly repents, owns their fault, and changes their ways—*for an extended period of time* (the more detrimental the offense, the longer it generally takes). A new track record of trustworthiness is what you're looking for. Start, for example, by praying that God would help you see a changed heart in your spouse. Watch for evidence over time. And move your heart forward: first, toward the idea of forgiveness;

and second, toward a decision to forgive. But we want to be clear: this is not done in blind faith. Watch for evidence of your partner's humility, repentance, and willingness to change their behavior and begin living up to their vows, and then take your steps of faith toward forgiveness and rebuilding trust.

This matter of rebuilding trust bears repeating to the offending partner: assuming you are genuinely sorry and striving to rebuild your relationship, the process through these emotional spaces is a very long one. You cannot be impatient or demanding. You have earned distrust and you must earn renewed trust. Essentially what is required for that to even be a possibility is a new track record from you of trustworthy behavior—of faithfulness. Trust can't be based on who you were prior to the offense, or a short season of "not betraying anymore." You must prove to be a person of integrity, honor, and fidelity—and do so over an extended period. Give them a reason to trust you, even as they work on finding the courage to risk doing so. At times this fragile process is one step forward, three steps back (one reason we highly recommend letting a therapist guide you through). At others, it's two steps forward and one step back. But throughout, your conviction must be *living in faithfulness, not going back.*

No matter the ocean in which you swim, the four steps help you live in self-control. Practice them and look for trusted others to support you on your journey.

NEW SELF, PEACEFUL US CONVERSATION:

- If a blended family couple, you may have other relationship pain cycles, for example, between former spouses or between a stepparent and child. What other pain cycles are pressing on you currently?
- If dating, what are the circumstances of your relationship that need attention?
- If parenting, what are the current issues that trigger dysregulation in your children or you?
- If you are facing a particular season of difficulty, how can you apply self-regulation to the situation?
- If trust has been damaged significantly in your relationship, what insights did the chapter give you as you survey the status of your relationship?

CHAPTER 11

Humility and the Four Steps in All Your Relationships

Issues of identity (being loved), safety (trust), and our pain cycle are not limited to conflict in marriage. In this chapter, we'll extend what you've learned to your sex life and help you apply the principles to other key relationships to see how humility, the four steps, and your peace cycle can positively impact them, too.

IN PARENTING

I came home one day and announced to Nan and my then-twenty-year-old son, "What I know about me is that I've had a very stressful day and I'm in a lousy mood. I just want you to know that because I'm trying desperately not to take it out on any of you—something I have been guilty of in the past. Just thought I'd give you a heads-up on what's going on with me. I'm not being quiet because of any irritation with you. It's been a hard day."

I've learned two things about this kind of everyday humility and modified four-step statement. First, my family appreciates it when I own my moods and they give me a little grace with it. In the past I didn't, and they felt responsible for Dad's grumpiness. They weren't. Second, saying things like this aloud makes it harder for me to be grumpy. It stops my pain cycle, holds me accountable, and empowers me with self-control.

And by the way, repeated demonstrations like this teach children self-control, too.

Terry Hargrave would tell you that he is an "on-time, pick up after yourself, and do your job" type of guy. These are not just annoying habits that he picked up haphazardly throughout his life. They were part of his survival. Terry came from a family that was physically and emotionally abusive. It was not like things were abusive for Terry 24/7, but the problem was he could never tell when things—even trivial things—would set off an out-of-control action by one of his parents. Three times out of five not hanging up a towel after a shower would not be a big deal. But the other two times, it would ignite a verbal berating from one of his parents accusing him of not caring, not appreciating them, and being useless. Rarer, but still a possibility, it might also set off a beating to the face and neck with the towel that he'd just left on the floor. His home, like many homes that carry a legacy of abuse, would be unpredictably out of control enough to drill into his emotions so that he never knew when, how, or why things would suddenly explode into violence. Because he never knew exactly when or why, he came to realize that it might happen at any time or at any place. As a result, he grew up always on guard to do the right thing to, perhaps, avoid abuse.

By age three Terry learned how to get himself out of bed in the morning, get himself dressed, fix his breakfast and lunch, and get himself out the door—and out of the way— to whatever play or school that was on the agenda. His parents called him a loner, and in some ways that was true. But he was not a loner because he did not want to have friends or be loved. He was a loner because he was protecting himself from interactions that might go badly for him. Yes, he felt unloved by his parents, but more important, when it came to the abuse, he felt chronically unsafe. So, he learned how to manage himself in such a way that people could find little fault with him or have an excuse to come after him. In short, he learned how to be an "on-time, pick up after yourself, and do your job" type of a guy. It was an essential part of his plan for survival.

Fast-forward thirty-five years, to when he and Sharon were raising their two children. Long before knowing about his own neurological ruts or developing the principles of Restoration Therapy, he still practiced the performance-based actions of being timely and doing things in a responsible way. Teaching his children how to be on time and pick up after themselves was not just an important training moment; to him, it was something essential to be done right. Even though he was far past being threatened with his safety over things being done right, he still managed to carry the intensity of how things *should* be done. After all, he would reason, these are responsible things that children should know! It was that intensity—that singular focus of how it *should* be done—that lead him to be far too hard on his son and daughter. They knew that being on time, doing chores, and hanging up towels was important to Terry, but they were always baffled about why it was such a big deal. And the harder he pushed, the more confused they were. His coping kicked in and he got angry.

Even from a distance you and I could understand how Terry's pain cycle was activated when he was young, and how he carried the intense feeling that things must be done right and on time into adulthood—and into parenting. He was never physically abusive to his children, but his anger did threaten and demean their identities and senses of safety.

Many years have gone by, and his children are adults. He has apologized for being far too angry at them over unimportant things as they were growing up and through the four steps, he, too, has gained some charge over his reactivity. But he still carries an intensity and anger in his pain cycle. He's still working on this. Just like you and me.

Parenting triggers our pain cycles. Nan and I have adult children, too, and we are still learning to parent *ourselves*. No matter the age of your children, there is eternal value in nurturing and connecting with your child's sense of worth (identity) and sense of safety—and managing *your* dysregulation.

What a dysregulated child needs most is a self-regulated parent. You can't control your children any more than you can your spouse. When a child is misbehaving, manage your own pain, get centered in truth, and respond accordingly. That's the best gift you can give a child at that moment. Don't join your child in blame/shame/control/escape behavior.

Instead, show them what it looks like to bring calm self-control to the moment. From peace we offer them peace.

At that point, we are coregulating our child. You'll remember from chapter 7 that coregulation is appropriate for parent-child relationships and instructional for their maturation process. We need to let our kids borrow our self-control until they can do that for themselves. In the meantime, in addition to modeling self-regulation, we can coach them toward understanding their pain and peace cycles. For example, after watching a child react to social situations with friends, ask questions that help them "chase their pain" so they can connect how painful emotions move them toward poor coping behavior.

"I noticed you picking at your friends during the sleepover. I'm wondering what you were feeling just before that. [Pause and listen.] Could you have been feeling a little left out, like you didn't belong? [This relates to matters of identity.] Tell me about that." You don't have to map their pain cycle on paper necessarily; just talking about it helps them connect the dots. "And what do you find yourself doing when you feel like you don't matter?"

Then you turn the corner. "Now, when friends ignore you, is it true that you don't matter? What would God say about that? What would I tell you about how unique and important you are? What if you remembered that when you're with your friends—how might that show itself in how you behave?"

Imagine having a few versions of this conversation with your child repeatedly throughout their childhood. Eventually, the truth can take root and they can shift from coregulation with you to self-regulation for the rest of their life. Your child and their spouse will thank you later.

IN LEADERSHIP

Let me challenge every leader reading this book: Make the humility shift often in your managerial role. Say, "What I know about me..." and use the four steps when you get frustrated, angry, or anxious in your role. Show people how to walk in humility by walking that way yourself...and see if you don't find them full of grace for you and the work you do together. You are learning to be humble in your marriage; apply the same skills to your leadership role and watch how it transforms your influence.

We think it's fair to say that over the past decade there has been a surge of leaders of all kinds who lead from a posture of pride and arrogance. From politicians, to executives, to pastors, there is an epidemic of pride at the top of many organizations, and it often leads to their downfall. And the public falls of these leaders, especially ministry leaders, has destroyed trust and made people feel unsafe, within the church and at times, with God. Ironically, it's the big personality of many leaders that people are drawn to and why they become megachurch pastors or megarich entrepreneurs to begin with. But without humility, they will, just as we do in marriage, remain blind to their own desires, pain, and poor ways of coping—and that will eventually lead to a fall.

Why?

In chapter 8, we introduced you to the principle repeated

throughout scripture that God opposes the proud and gives grace to the humble. First Peter 5:5 echoes the principle to both the shepherds and the sheep of a local congregation to whom Peter was writing. Both the leaders and the followers were admonished to clothe themselves with humility toward one another. Human relationships, we believe, are governed by the same principle that governs our vertical relationship with God. Pride invites opposition from others, while humility invites grace.

It is inevitable that prideful leaders are eventually rejected by their constituents, congregants, or shareholders because of their arrogance. Proverbs 29:23 says, "One's pride will bring him low, but he who is lowly in spirit will obtain honor" (ESV). Jesus said it this way, "For everyone who exalts himself will be humbled, and he who humbles himself will be exalted" (Luke 14:11 ESV). Pride will undo us. It's built into relationships. But humility invites a softening of those you lead (and from your spouse and other family members close to you). They are more patient with your faults, more understanding of your inadequacies, more long-suffering with your deficits. In a word, they have grace.

Imagine a leader, whether a pastor or politician, who never admits when they're wrong and who blames everyone else for what doesn't go right. Doesn't opposition rise inside you toward that person? Aren't you impatient with them? It's hard to like them when they walk around looking down on everyone else.

On the other hand, it's easy to give a second chance to a humble leader, one who admits their mistakes, owns their failings, and with a listening, caring ear invites input from the people. A pastor who is vulnerable from the pulpit with their temptations and struggles is someone you want to be around; they're someone you want to follow. But an arrogant, "how lucky you are to have me in your life" leader is someone you won't miss when they're gone.

This isn't rocket science. The principle is simple and clear, although it is difficult sometimes to discern pride from confidence. Strong leaders believe they can lead, but they know who God is and who they are not. And at the end of the day, they know they aren't any different than every other person under their charge. They, too, need a Savior. And they, too, need a Lord.

When James and John were posturing for second and third position in Christ's Kingdom, Jesus hit their pride hard. You know there are leaders who "lord it over" their people, Jesus says. "But it shall not be so among you. But whoever would be great among you must be your servant, and whoever would be first among you must be slave of all" (Mark 10:43-44 ESV). And then Jesus makes it clear that even He did not come to be served, but to serve and give His life away. Leadership, He essentially says, begins and ends with humility and being a servant. (For free bonus material about the pride/humility dynamic, visit rondeal.org/themindfulmarriage.)

IN FRIENDSHIPS

Because of a number of painful childhood experiences, Sharon Hargrave was so afraid of loneliness she pushed people away to protect herself.

Sharon grew up in a fun and loving family in southern California. She was the fourth of four children, the only girl with three older brothers. Their family built memories, played games together, and experienced the thrills of Disneyland! As a toddler Sharon remembers feeling prized and deeply loved by her family, being showered with kisses and hugs by her parents and brothers. But unfortunately, she also learned that life was fleeting and not trustworthy. When she was three years old, her father, who suffered from bipolar disorder before there was effective treatment, took his own life during a severe depressive episode, leaving her mother to raise four children. Her mom subsequently moved the family to Texas to be near her brother. Eighteen months later, Sharon's eldest brother rapidly became ill and died of acute leukemia. But the string of tragedies in her family was not over. Nine years later her next oldest brother, who was away at college, went missing. He and his date were found murdered and locked away in the trunk of his car.

Within a decade, her happy loving family of six was reduced to three in particularly disturbing and tragic ways. In the end, Sharon retained loving relationships with her mother and one remaining brother. But nothing felt safe. Throughout her teen years and into adulthood, Sharon understandably found it very difficult to trust life, friendships, even her husband. Everything felt fragile, and things and people she cared about unsafe. To cope, Sharon relied on control and criticism.

The reality of the effects of this coping stepped into her life again when she was about forty years old. She says she will never forget that week because it changed her life forever.

Sharon was the director of Vacation Bible School at their home church in Amarillo, Texas. From her viewpoint, she says, it was the best run VBS in the history of the world. They had more kids coming than ever before, a grand pool of volunteers that were fitted uniquely to their jobs, and she and her team had changed the schedule to make everything run smoothly. And then it happened.

She was striding through the preschool wing of the VBS when her codirector called across the hall, "Hey Sharon, quit acting like a pit bull with PMS!" The codirector laughed. Sharon laughed. But her heart fell into her stomach. Up until that moment, she thought everyone had loved her leadership at VBS. The only person she thought had trouble with her controlling nature was her husband, Terry, and his issues with her "superior organizational skills" (as Controllers might call them), was about him.

That same afternoon, she got a phone call from a good friend. To protect her feelings, the friend called to tell her that the next day she and several of her other friends were going to be invited into a women's organization that was *by invitation only*. She was calling Sharon to tell her why they thought she wouldn't want to be included. Whether Sharon wanted to be invited or not, it was obvious everyone else was included and it was painful she was not. Sharon held most of these friends at a distance so when it came to choosing who they wanted around them, she was out.

Being left alone in the world was her deep fear. Although she didn't put words to it and didn't acknowledge it, this experience helped her know how deep the pain ran in her life.

But at that point she didn't understand the pain or how that pain drove her to react. She feared that the world was unsafe and that people (as hard as they might try) could never promise her the future. Her pain story led her to try to control people when they didn't act the way she needed them to act. Both the week of VBS and not getting an invitation to the women's organization made her realize she needed to learn to be different in relationships. She wanted to learn to have fun, be open, and to be relaxed, and not just be in charge and give direction. Her reaction to keep the world safe by way of control had resulted in her feeling isolated.

Because of God's great love, she had been surrounded by people in her church, youth camp, Young Life, Navigators, and more who loved her. She hid her deep pain from them. Her testimony brought people into her life who empathized with her and gathered around her, but she kept them from knowing the real her.

She says, "I had embraced the message, somehow, that trauma should not affect Christians. That because of Christ in my life, the pain should not be present. What I know today is that the pain was very present but had masked itself in how I coped by controlling and being critical which, in essence, pushed people away creating more pain. The messages I tell myself and the ways I cope with that pain determine how others feel in my presence. Being in a place of peace does not mean that I won't feel pain. It does mean that I will be able to acknowledge my pain and learn how to cope in open, constructive ways that allow for connection and vulnerability."[1]

Another challenge related to Sharon's pain arose a few

years before the writing of this book. The Lord brought a new friend into her life to carry on the work Sharon had done in a ministry for church leaders. Her friend thinks about issues differently than Sharon does and sets about developing curriculum in a different way. When the friend creates a new handout or changes things to make it better, Sharon feels a bit unsafe or inadequate. Her friend is also connected with Sharon's former colleagues, and as a result Sharon noticed that she sometimes feels alone or on the outside.

"I have a choice," says Sharon. "I can calm myself by realizing that I am not alone, and in fact, this transition has brought a brilliant, caring woman into my life. When she changes things, I can blame others for the work we did before, feel horrible about who I am and shame myself, and continue to try to control what she does. Or I can stop, look at my pain, and see that I feel alone and unsafe. When I get centered in the truth that I am not alone, know that I am adequate, and that the work that God has allowed me to do has been meaningful to many, I can let go and move forward in a positive, Spirit-driven, life-giving way. This gives me the freedom to stay connected to the work that has meant so much to me and develop a new, life-giving relationship with my friend. The choice is mine."

IN YOUR SEX LIFE

If being emotionally naked feels vulnerable, being physically and sexually naked most certainly pushes our sense of vulnerability and safety. Now, having said that, it is also entirely possible to be completely naked and engaged in sexual activity with our spouse and not be naked at all. You can be naked physically and completely "clothed" at the same time, hiding who you are. People do it all the time. They have sex with prostitutes and share nothing of who they are. They have one-night stands but never reveal themselves. And married couples have intercourse on a regular basis but refrain from looking into one another's eyes.

Making love, on the other hand, involves gazing into the eyes of the other and allowing them to look deeply into yours all while entrusting your most private parts to the other's care. It is seeing and being seen. This requires two partners with a great deal of security in their identity and a strong sense of emotional safety with their usness. Together, the two pillars of love ("I am worthy") and safety ("I can trust you with my body, heart, and soul") create the context within which mutual surrender, peaceful vulnerability, and unrestrained pleasuring can take place. Not many couples achieve this kind of lovemaking because they haven't worked on the two pillars of their identity and safety enough; most couples just have sex. Consider yourself challenged to pursue the kind of passionate self-regulating lovemaking that God invites you to enjoy.

We are made for sexual pleasure. Sexuality is built into our very design—a tangible experience of God. Sex *is a wonder*. *A mystery* and a privilege to cherish and protect. A celebration of all that is good and holy. It is *deeply intimate*—for it touches the Divine! No wonder it brings ecstatic pleasure and has the potential to cause crushing pain.

And no wonder the evil one works hard to distort sex. Through, for example, pornography that distorts the brain, the mind, and the heart, and through shame, which makes us hide instead of feeling safe so we can see and be seen within sex. Satan wants you having sex *without* revealing yourself. Shame does that very efficiently. Traumatic experiences also distort the beauty of sexuality and steal our joy; they teach us not to trust ourselves to another person. And finally, Satan distorts marital sexuality with misinformation. Many sexual difficulties can be resolved with a little good information. Not locker room talk, pornography, or erotic novel information, but Bible-based, research-informed, balanced understandings of good sex (of which there are many good books to choose from).

Much of this distortion comes together in your pain cycle. In fact, your sexual relationship is often an intensely intimate expression of your couple pain cycle. If you struggle to trust your partner outside the bedroom, it will be difficult to get completely emotionally naked with them inside the bedroom. Oh, you'll have sex. But you won't find "naked and unashamed" in the bedroom unless you are working toward love and trust throughout your marriage.

Because your sexual relationship is tied to your overall pain and peace cycles, you will find that sex can trigger intense identity and safety pain, become a form of poor coping (e.g., makeup sex as a form of anxious pursuit of your partner), or be an amazing pleasurable expression of two mature, self-regulating partners with a strong usness.

And there's something else. Our identity and sense of safety are uniquely tied into sexual intimacy; couples can have unique pain cycles in the context of their sexuality. By "unique" we don't mean totally disconnected from their larger couple pain cycle, but distinct in that it seems to have its own pain elements that need attention.

Andre and Shantae sought help for their sex life. Andre initiated sex most of the time in their relationship. However, early in their relationship Shantae seemed just as interested in sex as he did; in fact, she often playfully initiated lovemaking. When that changed a few years into their marriage, Andre mistakenly interpreted her lack of desire for sex as a lack of desire for him. This tapped his identity pain stemming back to childhood; the cumulative pain story his brain repeated was that he wasn't worth pursuing. He experienced several disappointments from important people as a child, including the divorce of his parents that led to his father's rare involvement in his life. No matter how much he pursued his dad, his dad didn't pursue him.

Now married, Andre sexually pursued Shantae with blame, control, and escape. He tried to change her level of desire by pursuing sex more often and with creative enticements, by commenting on and criticizing her lack of desire for sex ("Why don't you want me anymore?"), and by analyzing when and how she was interested from time to time. He looked for her sexual "recipe" to control what ignited hunger for sex in her heart and tried to make that happen on his timetable. When all of that failed, Andre escaped into pornography. This is a common sexual escape for both men and women these days. Wrestling with differing sexual desires and an active pain cycle is hard; porn is easy. Stepping out of pride and into humility is hard; escape is easy.

Analyzing yourself instead of your spouse is hard; retreating into a "friend" that never disappoints—and never demands anything—is easy.

One of the lies of pornography is that a man who knows what to do can make any woman—even a sexually uninterested woman—want sex and scream with pleasure when she experiences it. That lie, coupled with Andre's sense of unworthiness of love, led to a pervasive fear that he wasn't adequate as a man.

More misinformation fueled Andre's pain. He believed that since Shantae's level of desire for sex shifted from high to low, that she no longer wanted sex or him. That conclusion is based on a common misunderstanding of desire. As our friend and researcher Dr. Michael Sytsma points out, there is more than one kind of desire.[2] When referring to how much someone wants sex, most people are speaking of **initiating desire**. What they are really asking is how often do you come hungry for sex, that is, have an internal drive that has you aroused and pursuing sex. Both men and women have high initiating desire early in relationships, but women often shift to what's called **receptive desire**. That's when you might not have felt hungry for sex, but when your partner says, "Hey, how about we grab something to eat?" you think, *Okay. I wasn't hungry for sex a minute ago, but now that you've brought it up, I can go for that.* Both initiating desire and receptive desire *are* desire. And both should be credited as "want." Andre was misinterpreting Shantae's shift in desire as "not wanting" when it wasn't. He just needed to adjust his expectations of who would initiate sex more often (him) and who would join him later (her). And what made him particularly vulnerable to this misinterpretation? His pain.

The narrative he carried since childhood that he wasn't worth loving and that people he loved would eventually leave.

Shantae used to say that her husband loved her more than life itself. But since their conflict over sex took center stage, she felt unsure. She began to think, *He wants sex, not me.* So, she pursued reassurance with requests like, "How come you don't text me anymore?" and "Do you still love me?"

Andre's criticism of Shantae's low sexual desire frustrated her sense of safety in the relationship, as did his use of pornography. *I'm not enough for him*, she thought (shame). *Next he'll probably turn to another woman.* In anxiety, she began to accommodate him sexually doing whatever she guessed would keep him close. All the while she felt disconnected from him and anxious while having sex; her accommodation was more of a coping strategy than an act of making love. At some level she knew their connection was phony. The manufactured, porn-star-like performance might have placated him for a while, but it left her feeling more unsafe and vulnerable.

Both partners started to explore their side of the sexual pain cycle and put words on their pain and coping. That, coupled with steps 3 and 4, led them to a peace cycle they are pursuing together. For example, Andre knew he had to stop looking at porn. As he did, a new strand of trust began to develop between him and Shantae. In addition, once Andre realized that her desire simply took a different expression from his—one of open responsiveness to him initiating sex—he experienced her desire and was able to attune to her and enjoy sex more. He stopped keeping a ledger of who initiated sex and who didn't, trusting the outcome. This, also, helped him trust that when she said, "Not now," it did not

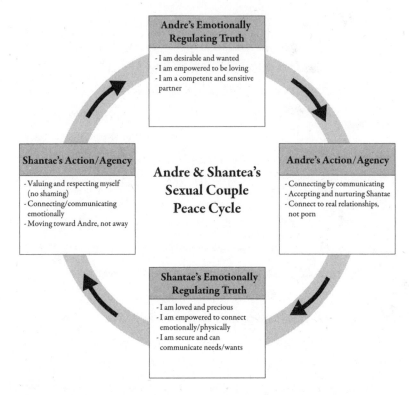

Illustration 6: Andre and Shantae's Sexual Couple Peace Cycle

mean she didn't love him. In turn, Shantae came to trust that Andre could self-soothe if, for whatever reason, she needed a rain check on a sexual invitation. She saw him as a man capable of waiting and saw herself as an empowered woman who could later consciously activate her energy for sex when it was an authentic expression of her love for him.

Your sexual pain cycle is always a subset of your couple pain cycle, and sometimes it's the same. But given how intimate sexuality is in marriage, it's worth asking if there are unique aspects of your sex life that need attention.

IN GRIEF

Sorrow comes to all of us. If you've ever loved anything or anyone, you've likely experienced loss (and if you haven't, you will). Our western culture is funny about grief. It's often seen as a problem to solve. But since grief and sorrow—especially those created by significant, intense losses—are tears of liquid love, you don't ever get past it, find closure, or go back to being who you were before the loss. It is a pain we carry, to one degree or another, throughout our lives.

We told you earlier that in 2009 we lost our middle son, Connor, when he was twelve years old. An MRSA staph infection ravaged his body over a ten-day period. We don't know how he contracted the bacteria, but it cut short his precious life. We've spoken about our journey publicly, so we won't take time to travel through that dark valley here, but I do want to share an observation that helped us wrestle with our grief and has helped others with theirs.

Around the first anniversary of Connor's death, we started to put words on our experience with grief. The ubiquitous five stages of grief from Elisabeth Kübler-Ross that everyone tossed at us had not described what we felt and had not given us any practical perspective by which to monitor our journey.

Instead, what we came to say was that in the wake of Connor's death our life seemed to be traveling on a train riding, as all trains do, on two rails. The left rail is sadness (deep, deep sadness) and the right rail, hope. The left rail gushes with anguish because we can't see him today;

the right includes the promise that we will see him again one day. The left, anger that we lost him and God didn't stop it; the right, trust that God knows what he's doing even if we don't. The left is empty yearning; the right is full of memories of an amazing young man who was creative, funny, and imaginative. The left, unspeakable sorrow that has recalibrated every aspect of our life; the right, peace in the arms of the suffering Savior who knows the depth of our sorrow because he's been there, done that.

And here's what we began to realize about the two rails: neither rail invalidates the other. Neither cancels the other. They coexist—and now, fifteen years later, we can tell you they still coexist... and will, it seems, till Jesus comes.

Let me pause a moment. Christians really need to understand that last part. We regularly judge one another for not moving past sadness, as if faith is all you need. No, faith informs my pain, but it does not erase my pain. The hope of seeing Connor again in heaven comforts me, but it doesn't stop my heart from hurting. Beauty can come out of ashes, but it doesn't incinerate the ashes. Please stop expecting yourself or your grieving friends to find acceptance, be okay, and stop hurting. It just doesn't work that way. Besides, sending that message to yourself or a grieving friend throws vinegar on their open wound. (See Proverbs 25:20.)

Grief is riding the two rails. Your whole life rests on them. Some days you're leaning almost entirely on the left rail of sorrow and pain—it's all you can see or feel, while other days you're balanced between both. Over time we tend to shift more to the right rail of hope, but the left is always there, too.

Nan and I began sharing this metaphor with other parents who had also lost a child, and they could relate. It just seemed to fit. And then, someone encouraged us to read the laments of scripture and the stories of God's people who experienced loss. We were stunned to learn just how many stories there are, from Job, to Lamentations, to Mary, Martha, and Jesus in John 11, to Jesus' experience in the Garden of Gethsemane. In addition, more than one-third of the Psalms are laments. Time and time again, we read of someone pouring out their heart and complaints to God—their anger, their depression, their debilitating sorrow, their confusion, and their doubt—then boldly asking God to act on their behalf, as they trust him with their circumstances. Wait, a good lament is composed of pain and trust? Doubt and faith? Weeping and turning to God? Those are the two rails. Certainly, our version of how this worked was much more muddled and unrefined than the scriptures, but boy, could we relate. Consider Psalm 77, for example.

> You [speaking to God] hold my eyelids open; I am so troubled that I cannot speak....
>
> "Will the Lord spurn forever, and never again be favorable? Has his steadfast love forever ceased? Are his promises at an end for all time? Has God forgotten to be gracious? Has he in anger shut up his compassion?" (Psalm 77:4, 7–9 ESV)

That sounds a whole lot like the left rail to me. Pain, pain, and more pain. And he's throwing it at God!

Then, he shifts to the right rail.

Then I said, "I will appeal to this, to the years of the right hand of the Most High. I will remember the deeds of the LORD; yes, I will remember your wonders of old." (Psalm 77: 10–11 ESV)

This is what we do in grief: we bring our pain to God, but then we let the truth of God, what we believe to be reliable and trustworthy about God, inform our pain about how to move forward.

As with all pain, then, the four steps can guide your journey in grief. Articulate the loss and what it means to you. Identify what coping actions you're undertaking to deal with your loss. And then recognize the right rail; let truth speak to your pain and tell you in steps 3 and 4 how to cope in faith. You will most certainly continue to ride the left rail (depending on the size of the loss, perhaps until you die), but the right rail will inform the expression of your grief along the way.

Since finding our own words for our grief journey, we've learned that Kübler-Ross's research on grief was never intended to apply unilaterally to all kinds of grief (she studied people who were anticipating the death of a loved one) and she never intended her descriptive model of grief to become a prescription for how to grieve well. (We really should stop repeating the five stages to one another as if that's what good grief looks like.)

Today, the more readily accepted model of grief is called the Dual Process Model of Coping with Bereavement, and it suggests that there are two major aspects of good grieving: loss-oriented aspects and restoration-oriented aspects.

Loss-oriented elements focus on grieving, the many emotions that surround the sadness, and wrestling with the reality of the loss. Restoration-oriented elements have to do with walking forward in life, that is, doing new things, attending to life as it now is, stepping away from the intensity of grief from time to time, learning new roles, and building new relationships. Loss-oriented aspects look back while Restoration-oriented aspects look forward.[3]

Do you see it? Those two elements of the model, essentially, describe the two rails. One is focused on sorrow and the past, and the other is a reorientation to living in the present, given what is true. One comes with tears, the other with new beginnings and hope. And it's the vacillating movement between the two, the researchers say, that adds up to good grief. Being sad one moment and hopeful the next. Telling stories and looking at videos that bring a flood of tears one minute and letting your trust in God inform your pain the next.

Find support for your grief journey with resources like GriefShare or, for bereaved parents like us, whilewerewaiting.org.

NEW SELF, PEACEFUL US CONVERSATION:

- Consider each section of this chapter. What jumped out to you as you applied humility and the four steps to your parenting, leadership roles, friendships, and/or sex life? (Take note of topics that you want to dedicate time to discuss soon.)

- What triggers you most in parenting? Put words on how this connects to your identity and/or sense of safety, as well as how it connects to your anxiety regarding your child's developing identity and sense of safety in the world.

- Can you think of humble leaders whom you would like to emulate? Who are the prideful ones and how do you see others or yourself opposing their leadership (e.g., rejecting, doubting, not voting for, etc.)?

- What are the core pains in your current friendships? Share how your spouse can support you while you learn to manage your pain differently.

- What are some unique pains connected to your sex life? Speak for yourself, talking about your pain and how it's tied to your larger pain story. If your sexual pain story or couple pain cycle feels too fragile to manage on your own, find a Christian sex therapist who can help (sexualwholeness.com).

- What's your coping pattern with sorrow or grief? Read Psalm 77 and notice the two rails the author speaks about. How might this inform your grief journey?

Everyday Humility

One morning Nan and I had a tense start to our day. Nan had brought up a conflict from a couple of days earlier. I told her it wasn't a good time (I was avoiding a tough subject) and asked her to wait till I could really focus on the topic. Years previously we agreed that when one of us asks for a "continuance" they are responsible to make the discussion happen within a reasonable time. I did not do that. When Nan brought it up again and asked if I was ever going to get around to it (she felt like her pain was not important to me), I knew I had dropped the ball. Plus, I still didn't want to talk about the issue. We both reacted out of our pain and, pridefully, focused on what the other person needed to change.

Then, on the way to work, we simultaneously sent text messages. Mine said, "I am praying that the Lord would awaken my heart to the fear I have in bringing up things that might cause more angst and that I would be mindful of your need to close the loop on hard conversations. I'm sorry that I run away from those things. I know loving you well means I must work through that." Nan's said, "My daily prayer is that I die to my selfishness, pride, and root of unforgiveness. I did not love you with patience, kindness, and self-control this morning. I was arrogant, rude, and brought up your past. You are spot-on about how I see and talk about your work. I compare and have unresolved resentment. I am asking God to heal that and bridle my tongue. For that, I'm sorry. I'm a work in progress. I love you."

Now, what do you think happened in each of us when we read what amounted to the other's humility shift? We softened. Perhaps even you found yourself softening toward us as you read our messages. When someone becomes vulnerable with their pain and reactivity and takes ownership of who they are (or were) and who they need to become, it naturally invites grace from the other. Again, it doesn't guarantee an *immediate* softening of the other's heart; sometimes the pain is so significant, it does not melt easily or quickly. But in general, humility creates a climate where softening, patience, and grace is more likely.

The journey of discipleship is lifelong. Every day we strive to die to ourselves, and the next morning our pride and old self resurrect. Coming to follow Christ in humility is the right first step. And the middle step. And the last step. Putting on humility in between those steps takes lots of prayer, Spirit-empowered strength, and self-control.

What I know about Nan and me is that we have always loved each other. We've always been sexually faithful to each other. And we've always had the best of intentions toward one another in our marriage. Even so, emotional dysregulation is real. RT taught us how, by God's grace, to renew our minds.

Nan and I are, well, still imperfect. We still get dys-regulated. But we know what to do when it happens. The effects are often short-lived if not avoided altogether. And slowly but surely, one mindful practice after another, we are becoming new. Becoming one.

Acknowledgments

Ron and Nan Deal

Our renewed usness is a testimony to the mercy of God. We are deeply grateful to Him for it and taste it afresh each and every morning.

We are thankful to our agent, Chip MacGregor, for his expertise and coaching throughout this project. And to Jenny, Ami, and the Worthy Books family, thank you for your partnership and making this book more approachable.

And finally, we are so grateful for the family and friends who have stood beside us through thick and thin. Your love and care sustained us in the darkest nights and helped show us the light of dawn.

Terry and Sharon Hargrave

We are thankful to the Restoration Therapy community of therapists, coaches, pastors, colleagues, and friends who have shared this model with others countless times. Your diligence in sharing these concepts have continued to inspire us about the lasting change and the many applications we can make for those who choose to self-regulate, be mindful of their own actions, and work to engage with those around them in a healthy and meaningful way.

Resources

Find Bonus Content, Host an Event with Ron and Nan Deal, Attend a Livestream

The Mindful Marriage Conference | Grieving Child Loss | Smart Stepfamily Seminars

rondeal.org/themindfulmarriage

For Marriages in Crisis (The Hideaway Experience) or to Find an RT Therapist

intensives.com | restorationtherapytraining.com/find-a-therapist

For Professional Counselors and Therapists

Restoration Therapy Training

restorationtherapytraining.com

For Professional Coaches and Church Leaders

Restoration Coaching

restorationtherapytraining.com

**For Small Group Material for Churches (consistent with
The Mindful Marriage principles)**

RelateStrong for Couples

boonecenter.pepperdine.edu

For Resources Related to Mental Health Concerns

RelateStrong Leadership Series

boonecenter.pepperdine.edu

**For Blended Family Couples, Counselors, &
Ministry Leaders**

smartstepfamilies.com | familylife.com/blended

Appendix 1

The Humility Shift Daily Exercise

When you intentionally choose humility and practice it daily, you can emotionally self-regulate. Triggering makes you feel like an out-of-control automobile screaming down the highway at one hundred miles per hour. You get angry, become controlling, shame yourself, and/or escape and run away—sometimes all four—in a cascade of emotion, totally focused on what *someone* has done that has been insulting or insufficient to you feeling loved (who you are) or emotionally safe ("Can I trust you?"). Your heart will lie to you—telling you that it is your spouse, friend, child, boss, *someone other than you* who is responsible for what you feel and how you are reacting. *They are the ones that are wrong and need to change and I am right in the way I feel and the way I am acting.* When this happens, you need to exit your emotional dysregulation at the next ramp. You need to slow down and see yourself rightly. Self-soothe and manage your emotions and your own pain to cultivate peace.

One way to get more accustomed with this "slow down and exit" is to daily remind yourself of the truth. Doing this on a regular basis helps rewire your brain to respond out of truth instead of pain. Every person will benefit from taking a few minutes each day to repeat this simple Humility Shift statement. Persons who have experienced little love and trustworthiness in their life or who have been the victims of traumatic violations of their identity and safety will need to practice this humility shift with more intentionality to override their pain cycle.

This is not something you just say; you are *creating* a new story *about yourself* rooted in truth. Posture your heart to be open to the work of the Holy Spirit and prepare yourself to enact the four steps in dysregulated moments during your day.

Read the following Humility Shift Daily Exercise out loud daily (or until it becomes a natural part of you). It will show you how to renew your mind. Be transformed. Become a living sacrifice of love and trustworthiness.

The Humility Shift Daily Exercise
(2 minutes)

1. REMEMBER YOUR GOAL. Read the following aloud.

Put on then, as God's chosen ones, holy and beloved, compassion-ate hearts, kindness, humility, meekness, and patience, bearing with one another and, if one has a complaint against another, forgiving each other; as the Lord has forgiven you, so you also must forgive. And above all these put on love, which binds everything together in perfect harmony. And let the peace of Christ rule in your hearts, to which indeed you were called in one body. And be thankful. (Colossians 3:12–15 ESV)

2. PROCLAIM TRUTH ABOUT GOD IN YOUR LIFE. Raise your open hands at arm's length toward heaven and say some truths about God and God's nature, being, and character aloud.

For example: *God is the Creator, the Authority over all, Perfect and Loving, and has a Specific Plan for me. God is More, I am Less.*

If you'd like, write your own statement here:

_____

_____

_____

3. SAY THE TRUTH ABOUT YOURSELF AND HOW GOD SEES YOU. Lower your open hands and place them over your heart and say some truths about yourself that God says about you OUT LOUD.

For example: *I am Special, Chosen, Holy and Beloved by God who Sacrificed All for me. I am Loved Like No Other.*

Using the truths from your peace cycle (page 99), write your own statement here:

_____

_____

_____

(continued)

4. RECKON WITH YOUR CURRENT REBELLION THROUGH OUT-OF-CONTROL EMOTIONAL DYSREGULATION. Lower both open hands to your sides and let your head drop downward and state the reality of what you are feeling and doing in comparison to the Colossians passage you read above OUT LOUD.

For example: *My old self moves against God and who I am Created to be. My heart often rejects the fruits of the Spirit. I do not have the compassionate heart that God gave to me, and I struggle with humility and patience.*

Write your own statement here:

_____

_____

_____

5. RELEASE THE DRIVE TO BE REACTIVE AND EMBRACE SELF-REGULATION AND GROWTH. Either place your open hands on your opposite shoulders (cross arms) or take a knee to the ground holding your hands open and say what your next step is OUT LOUD.

I chose the path of humility and will slow down and repent of my blame, shame, control, and/or escape reactivity. Instead, I will do my four steps and move my heart to be self-controlled, patient, and humble.

Appendix 2

If You Have Experienced Abuse

Your story of pain may currently include someone, either male or female, who is threatening your safety or the safety of those in your home. That could look like sexual or physical abuse, where someone molests or hits you or someone in the home, or is physically intimidating (e.g., throws things or punches holes in the wall). It could be emotional abuse, where the person makes you feel dumb, withholds money from you, or controls your interactions with other people. It could be that you are living with an addict who rages, is using up all your life savings, or continues to abuse porn, drugs, alcohol, gambling—or a host of other addictive substances. You could be in a relationship with someone who is having an active affair and refuses to give it up. Or your lack of safety may come from trying to stay in a relationship with someone who is emotionally unstable, perhaps with a mental health diagnosis that, unless treated, causes them to act in ways that threaten your well-being, your life, or the lives of your children.

We believe this book can teach you how to self-regulate

so that when you are making tough decisions about how to handle these very difficult life situations, you can do so from a calm, thoughtful place and not a place of dysregulation. In addition, recognizing the truth of your value will help you to see that you are worth more than this person's behavior would imply and, we hope, empower you to pursue physical and emotional safety.

If you are in an abusive situation, don't focus on your couple pain cycle. Instead, focus on your individual pain cycle (see chapter 5) and the four steps (see chapter 8). In other words, focus on your pain, how you react, the truth of your worth, and how new self-care actions on your part can move you out of harm's way and into a place of safety. From there, you will make much better decisions about the relationship you have been in.

We also suggest you surround yourself with a therapist and mature Christians who can encourage you as you seek safety and walk out new boundaries. Christian counselors and organizations can be found online. Therapists familiar with the principles of this book can be found at restoration therapytraining.com/find-a-therapist.

Appendix 3

Exercises 1–5 (Extra Copies)

A marital partner (or friend or family member) may want their own space to complete the exercises. Copies of each are provided here. Responses to exercises 4 and 5 can be transferred to the couple pain cycle on page 99.

Exercise 1

Identifying Emotions in Your Pain Cycle

1. When I am upset—unsettled, anxious, insecure—or triggered, how do I usually feel? An alternative question may be, What messages have I received about my worth, value, or importance from my spouse, family, or friends when I'm upset, and what emotions are connected to them?

Circle one or two emotions that best answer the question. If you circle more than two, put a star beside the emotions that are most common.

Unloved	Unworthy	Insignificant	Alone	Hopeless
Worthless	Devalued	Defective	Inadequate	Unappreciated
Rejected	Unaccepted	Unwanted	Abandoned	

Other: _____

The words you have circled usually pertain to the primary emotions associated with your IDENTITY when you are not feeling at peace (i.e., are upset or unsettled).

2. When I am emotionally upset or unsettled, how do I usually feel about the situation or relationship? An alternative question may be, what messages about relationships have I received from family or friends, and what emotions are tied to them?

Circle one or two words that best describe how you feel.

Unsafe	Unfair	Used	Guilty	Unsure
Fearful	Powerless	Controlled	Out of Control	Unknown
Vulnerable	Disconnected	Betrayed	Insecure	Not Enough

Other: _____

The words you have circled almost always pertain to the primary emotions associated with your sense of SAFETY when you are not feeling at peace (i.e., are upset or unsettled).

Exercise 2

Mapping Your Individual Pain Cycle

1. Look back at the feelings that you identified in Exercise 1 (page 202). Write those words in the first box of the Pain Cycle (page 204) under the title PAIN I FEEL.

2. Connect those emotions with the actions or coping responses from the list below. When you feel those emotions, how do you normally react? **Circle up to five *of the most common or consistent* reactions/coping that best describe what you do.**

Blames Others	Shames Self	Controls	Escapes / Creates Chaos
Rage	Depressed	Perfectionists	Impulsive
Angry	Negative	Performs	Numbs Out
Sarcastic	Whines	Judgmental	Avoids Issues
Arrogant	Inconsolable	Demanding	Escapes Using Substance
Aggressive	Catastrophizing	Critical	Escapes Using Activity
Retaliatory	Manipulative	Defensive	Irresponsible
Threatening	Fearful	Anxious	Selfish
Punishing	Pouting	Intellectualizes	Minimizes
Fault Finding	Harms Self	Nagging	Addicted
Discouraging	Needy	Lecturing	Secretive
Other: _____			

3. Write the words you've circled in the Pain Cycle under the title COPES/ REACTS (page 61).

4. Think about how people around you respond to you when you react in the ways described in the prior two sections. What do they usually say or do? Write up to five of those responses under the title OTHERS REACT in the Pain Cycle.

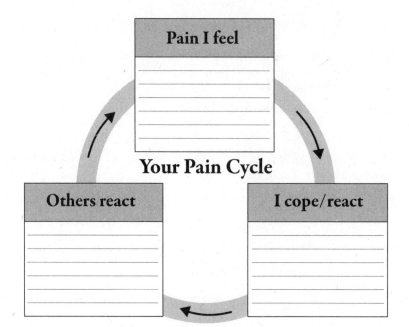

Your Pain Cycle

Mapping Your Couple Pain Cycle (see chapter 6)

Refer to your completed individual pain cycle (Exercise 2 above). Talk to your spouse and decide which of you will be Spouse #1 and which will be Spouse #2. Then, on page 74, record the words you both identified as PAIN I FEEL and how you COPE/REACT in the appropriate box.

Your spouse's responses will be recorded on that same page. If not, ask them to share what he or she identified in those same sections of their individual pain cycle and write those in the corresponding sections of the couple pain cycle.

(If each of you has a copy of this book and is recording your thoughts separately, decide which of you will be SPOUSE #1 and SPOUSE #2 so you can be consistent in your documentation of your pain cycle.)

Identifying Self-Regulating Truths

Think about the words that can emotionally regulate the painful lies about yourself, your identity, and your sense of safety. Which words below are meaningful and powerful to you because they represent the truth about your identity and safety? Choose words that directly repudiate the lies your pain cycle has been telling you.

(Circle three to five words that you would like to be able to claim as your own that would be representative of the new reality or truth about your identity and sense of safety.)

Loved	Worthy	Significant	Not Alone	Prized
Valuable	Precious	Adequate	Approved	Accepted
Wanted	Appreciated	Hopeful	Free	Safe
Secure	Sure	Fulfilled	Capable	Empowered
In Control	Protected	Connected	Intimate	Competent
Validated	Successful	Enough		

Other: _____

These words are your Emotionally Regulating Truths.

Exercise 5

New Actions Based on Truth (see chapter 7)

Look back at the truths you identified in Exercise 4. Concentrate on these words a bit and let the reality of these truths about your identity and safety soak in. Write down these words below so you can remember them easily.

_____

Talk to your spouse. On page 99, record the words you both identified as EMOTIONALLY REGULATING TRUTH from exercise 4 in the appropriate box (SPOUSE #1 or SPOUSE #2).

Now look at the list of words below that describe different actions/agency. When you are focused on the truth, what behaviors/actions would you likely take or choose to do? **(Circle two to five action/agency words that best describe what you would choose to do when you are in your truth and feel a sense of peace. Choose words that directly oppose the actions you take when you are in pain.)**

Loving	Values Self	Balanced Give/Take	Responsible
Encouraging	Respects Self	Vulnerable	Reliable
Supportive	Positive	Open	Self Controlled
Inclusive	Flexible	Engaging	Connected
Kind	Optimistic	Appreciative	Intimate
Listening	Hopeful	Gentle	Faithful
Accepting	Self-Aware	Relaxed	Forthcoming
Patient	Confident	Lets Things Go	Problem Solving
Compassionate	Affirming	Nurturing	

Other: _____

Record the words you circled above in your ACTION/AGENCY space on page 99. Talk to your spouse and record their words in their space.

Notes

Introduction

1. *The American Heritage Dictionary of the English Language*, 5th ed., accessed online at Wordnik, https://www.wordnik.com/words/mindful; *Merriam-Webster.com Dictionary*, https://www.merriam-webster.com/dictionary/mindful.
2. For more on Restoration Therapy and small group resources like Relate-Strong, see the ad page in the back of the book.

Chapter 1. Nurturing Your Usness

1. Daniel J. Siegel, *Mindsight: The New Science of Personal Transformation* (New York: Bantam Books, 2011).
2. Terry D. Hargrave and Franz Pfitzer, *Restoration Therapy: Understanding and Guiding Healing in Marriage and Family Therapy* (New York: Routledge, 2011), 180.
3. To be fair, recent research suggests that the part of the downstairs brain known as the amygdala, in addition to setting off alarms of perceived threat, is more sophisticated than it's often given credit for. It has, for example, demonstrated sophisticated computational properties and promotes intelligent decisions when the body is calm and relaxed. In normal everyday life, it very well may work alongside the prefrontal cortex in determining which goals are worth pursuing and formulating plans to achieve them. See M. L. Dixon and C. S. Dweck, "The Amygdala and the Prefrontal Cortex: The Co-construction of Intelligent Decision-Making," *Psychological Review* 129 no. 6 (2022), 1414–1441, http://dx.doi.org/10.1037/rev0000339.

4. Richard J. Foster, *Learning Humility: A Year of Searching for a Vanishing Virtue* (Downers Grove, IL: InterVarsity Press, 2022), 9–10.

Chapter 2. The Two Pillars of a Healthy Relationship: Love and Trust

1. Curt Thompson, as heard on the *Being Known Podcast*, https://being knownpodcast.com; see also Curt Thompson, "Spirituality, Neuroplasticity, and Personal Growth—Curt Thompson (Full Interview)," Biola University's Center for Christian Thought, March 7, 2013, https://cct .biola.edu/spirituality-neuroplasticity-and-personal-growth-curt-thompson -full-interview/.

2. Some Christians balk at this idea because it sounds like conditional love, and marriage, they say, should be unconditional. That's a very romantic idea, but it's not prudent or reasonable. Intuitively, these same people know they would not subject their children to a spouse who was a pedophile, nor be vulnerable with or trust an unfaithful and unrepentant spouse. (Some partners do choose to stay in these situations, but their trust of the partner will be very limited, and they will limit their emotional risks in the relationship.) Truly very few human relationships are unconditional. Even God doesn't require that of us in marriage; he allows for divorce, for example, when the most essential qualities of marriage, fidelity and faith in God, are broken in stubborn unrepentance (see Matt. 19:3–12 and 1 Cor. 7:15). Love is not unconditional. Said another way, love is conditioned on safety. Now, just to be clear, given that marriage is symbolic of God's love and faithfulness to us, it does have the high calling of lifelong commitment and selflessness—*unless* a spouse proves they are unwilling to repent from breaking their vows and return to a loving and trustworthy posture in the marriage. At that point, it seems reasonable to expect them to be untrustworthy and act accordingly.

Chapter 7. Choose to Emotionally Regulate

1. Suzanne Midori Hanna, *The Transparent Brain in Couple and Family Therapy: Mindful Integrations with Neuroscience* (New York: Routledge, 2014).

2. Rick Hanson, "Overcoming the Negativity Bias," Rich Hanson, Ph.D. (website), https://www.rickhanson.net/overcoming-negativity-bias/.

3. Terry D. Hargrave, Nicole E. Zasowski, and Miyoung Yoon Hammer, *Advances and Techniques in Restoration Therapy* (New York: Routledge, 2019), 90–92.

4. Stephen W. Porges and Seth Porges, *Our Polyvagal World: How Safety and Trauma Change Us* (New York: W. W. Norton, 2023), 78.

Chapter 8. The Path to Peace: The Four Steps

1. See Matthew 23:12, "Whoever exalts himself will be humbled, and whoever humbles himself will be exalted" (ESV).

2. See 1 Peter 5:5, "Clothe yourselves, all of you, with humility toward one another, for 'God opposes the proud but gives grace to the humble'" (ESV). We would add, *"And so do spouses!"*

3. Stephen W. Porges and Seth Porges, *Our Polyvagal World: How Safety and Trauma Change Us* (New York: W. W. Norton, 2023), 49.

4. Terry D. Hargrave and Franz Pfitzer, *Restoration Therapy: Understanding and Guiding Healing in Marriage and Family Therapy* (New York: Routledge, 2011), 157–169.

Chapter 9. Practicing the Four Steps

1. Stephen W. Porges and Seth Porges, *Our Polyvagal World: How Safety and Trauma Change Us* (New York: W. W. Norton, 2023), 18–19, 92.

2. James Swanson, *Dictionary of Biblical Languages with Semantic Domains: Greek (New Testament)* (Oak Harbor, WA: Logos Research Systems, 1997).

3. Terry D. Hargrave, Nicole E. Zasowski, and Miyoung Yoon Hammer, *Advances and Techniques in Restoration Therapy* (New York: Routledge, 2019), 167–168.

4. Stephen W. Porges and Seth Porges, *Our Polyvagal World: How Safety and Trauma Change Us* (New York: W. W. Norton, 2023), 49.

5. Learn more about the recovery ministry re:generation at "Re:generation," Watermark Resources, https://www.watermarkresources.com/ministries/regen.

Chapter 10. Peace for the Journey

1. Ron L. Deal and David H. Olson, *The Smart Stepfamily Marriage: Keys to Success in the Blended Family* (Bloomington, MN: Bethany House, 2015), 46.

2. Ron L. Deal and Gary Chapman, *Building Love Together in Blended Families: The 5 Love Languages and Becoming Stepfamily Smart* (Chicago, IL: Northfield Publishing, 2020), 22.

3. Learn more about the blended family ocean and ministering to stepfamilies at the Smart Stepfamilies website, https://smartstepfamilies.com.

4. See the work of Scott Stanley at *Sliding vs. Deciding: Scott Stanley's Blog*, https://slidingvsdeciding.blogspot.com/; Scott M. Stanley, Galena K. Rhoades, and Frank D. Fincham, "Understanding Romantic Relationships Among Emerging Adults: The Significant Roles of Cohabitation and Ambiguity" in *Romantic Relationships in Emerging Adulthood*, ed. Frank D. Fincham and Ming Cui (Cambridge, UK: Cambridge University Press, 2011), 234–251.

5. Terry Hargrave has authored books on caring for aging parents such as *Boomers on the Edge* (Grand Rapids, MI: Zondervan, 2009) and *Strength and Courage for Caregivers* (Grand Rapids, MI: Zondervan, 2008).

6. We recommend the ministry While We're Waiting, https://whilewerewaiting.org. Also, we made this video to help parents: "Can You Recover from Losing a Child? Marriage Advice with Ron and Nan Deal," YouTube, video, https://www.youtube.com/watch?v=jwC0xmKjccs.

7. Find an RT therapist at https://restorationtherapytraining.com/find-a-therapist.

8. Wendy Wang and Michael Toscano, "More Scrolling, More Marital Problems," Institute for Family Studies, July 26, 2023, https://ifstudies.org/blog/more-scrolling-more-marital-problems-. For more see David G. Myers, "Smartphones, Phubbing, and Relationship Satisfaction," Institute for Family Studies, February 2, 2023, https://ifstudies.org/blog/smartphones-phubbing-and-relationship-satisfaction.

Chapter 11. Humility and the Four Steps in All Your Relationships

1. Sharon Hargrave, personal communication, December 2023.

2. Shaunti Feldhahn and Dr. Michael Sytsma, *Secrets of Sex and Marriage: 8 Surprises That Make All the Difference* (Minneapolis: Bethany House, 2023).

3. See Margaret Stroebe and Henk Schut (1999) "The Dual Process Model of Coping with Bereavement: Rationale and Description, Death Studies," 23:3, 197–224, DOI: 10.1080/074811899201046.

About the Authors

Terry Hargrave, PhD, and Sharon Hargrave, LMFT, are the founders of Restoration Therapy. Terry served as the Evelyn and Frank Freed Professor of Marriage and Family Therapy at Fuller Theological Seminary and has been training therapists for more than thirty-five years. Sharon served as the executive director of the Boone Center for the Family at Pepperdine University, is the founder of RelateStrong, and maintains a therapy private practice. In their work together as authors, educators, conference speakers, retreat leaders, and trainers, they are passionate about helping people restore love and trust in marriages and families, and building close, intimate, and connected relationships. They reside in Arizona and have two adult married children and a growing number of grandchildren.

Ron Deal, MMFT, and Nan Deal, BSE, are popular conference speakers who lead The Mindful Marriage Conference, seminars for blended families, and facilitate a small group for parents who have lost a child. Frequently featured in national media, Ron is on staff at FamilyLife, the bestselling author of more than a dozen books and resources, a licensed marriage and family therapist, and host of the *FamilyLife Blended* podcast. Nan retired from teaching after twenty-five years and currently works for Live Thankfully. They have three sons, a daughter-in-law, one grandson, and a golden retriever. They reside in Little Rock, Arkansas. Learn more at rondeal.org.